ADVANCE PRAISE FOR 1

"Amparo puts into words decades of pra........ ...... useful experience in managing talent. She has a knack for defining how companies can attract, deploy, and engage talent in today's world. Her work is forward thinking and pragmatic."

Dave Ulrich
Rensis Likert Professor of Business, University of Michigan.
Partner, The RBL Group

"In today's highly connected world, more talent is being sourced virtually, yet many recruiters fall short on finding the best candidates. By reading Talent 3.0, you'll learn from Amparo exactly how to best use the Web to find the talent that will push your business forward."

Dan Schawbel
New York Times Bestselling Author of *Promote Yourself* and *Me 2.0*.

"Amparo's book, *Talent 3.0*, is an extensive and carefully arranged text, highlighting very significant and crucial tools for advancing the subject of Talent Management. It will certainly be a treasure for HR practitioners as well as academics who plan to improve their horizons on this important subject."

Dr. John Opute
Course Director, MSc International HR,
London South Bank University

"Attracting, developing and retaining talent in this hyper-connected world is no easy task. Amparo has put together what is needed for HR professionals and other management stakeholders to understand concepts and trends around this important topic."

Abdulla Zaid Al Shehhi
Head of International Expansion, Abu Dhabi Islamic Bank

"Amparo has a long and successful, both academic and business expertise, which makes her book a precious companion for a wide range of HR experts in today's world."

Carlos Espinosa de los Monteros
High Commissioner for Brand Spain. Ministry of Foreign Affairs

"The future of human capital is innovation and technology. Amparo is a guru in HR and her book gives us the keys to attracting new talent in a new international labour market. This is the new talent management 3.0."

Iñigo Sagardoy de Simón
President Sagardoy HR Lawyers

"Amparo is the epitome of what leading in the imagination age entails: creativity, drive, curiosity and determination. Her work is critical in guiding people and organisations to find talent in this new era."

Silvia Damiano
CEO About My Brain and author of *Leadership is Upside Down*

Talent
3.0

Amparo Díaz-Llairó
Foreword by Wim Focquet

Talent
3.0

LONDON   NEW YORK   SAN FRANCISCO   SHANGHAI
MEXICO CITY   MONTERREY   BUENOS AIRES
MADRID   BARCELONA   BOGOTA

LID Publishing Ltd
One Adam Street
London
WC2N 6LE
United Kingdom

31 West 34th Street, Suite 8004,
New York, NY 1001, US

info@lidpublishing.com
www.lidpublishing.com

A member of:

Printed in Spain

EAN-ISBN13: 978-1-907794-16-2
Translation: Don Topley
Correction: Cindy Hawes
Cover design: LID Editorial
Typesetting: produccioneditorial.com

First edition: December 2016

This book is specially dedicated to my mother Rosalina, my father Antonio, my brother Alfonso, my sister-in-law, Inés, and my two cute nephews Alfonso and Daniel, the next generation of talent.

Contents

Acknowledgements

LID publishing: Marcelino Elousa, Jeanne Bracken, Raúl López, Laura Díez, Don Topley and Cindy Hawes.

Foreword of this book: Wim Focquet

Endorsements: Dave Ulrich, Dan Schawbel, John Opute, Carlos Espinosa de los Monteros, Íñigo Sagardoy de Simón, Abdulla Zaid Al Shehhi, Silvia Damiano

Friends and colleagues: Isa Pueyo, Dani Sánchez, Víctor Sánchez, Irene Sánchez, Roser García, José Maria Carpena, Daniel Cordón, Arturo Díaz-Tejeiro, Saif Al Mansoori, Anita Wales, Joy Baruah, Riaan Baruah, Silvia Schania, Stefan, María Luisa Ruiz, Javi Ruano, David Ruano, Marta Ruano, Ethel Vasconcellos, Meritxell Martí, Rafa Moll de Alba, Eduard Sabaté, Sandra Esteban, Paula Sabaté, Marta Puigvert, Giorgio Avigo, Bruno Avigo, Michael Daniel, Glenn Kocher, Leila Hayat, Manuel Moratiel, Yasser Oukara, Sonia Fernández-Durán, Youssef Loukili, Sonsoles de Miguel, Manu Zamorano, Celes Rodriguez, Gema Zamorano, Susana Zabara, Gabriel Muñoz, Gabriel Schkolnik, Rosa Muñoz,

Nahid Tarah, Abraham Rodriguez, Urko Santamaría, Horacio Romero, Maria León, Gilles Ricart, Estela Muñoz, Teresa Martín de Vidales, Lucas Gómez, Felipe García-Bañón, Sara Bieger, Toni Pons, Eugenio Llamas, Mónica Piñero, Inés Aschl, Amarantha Pallás, Emily Pericás, Carmen Rodenas, Betty Tafalla, Andrea Gil, Ricardo Metón, Yolanda Tena, Felipe Tena, Cristina Calvo, Begoña Sáez, Carlos Lópes, Guillermo Lopes, Duarte Lopes, Rut Parella, Santi, Carla Muiños, Georgina Cisquella, Aniol Cisquella, Gal.la Cisquella, Susana de Jaen, Liza Santos, Adriana Domínguez, Alejandro Benaroch, Bruno Mazzili, Marco Saetta, Mariana Cara, Eva Garcia, Maribel Bofill, Juanma Romero, Leonor Nieva, Esther Romero, Lorena, Noelia Narro, María Rueda, Paula Márquez, Raghya Choukri, Óscar El Hadri, Pilar Gómez-Acebo, Nuria Chinchilla, Pilar Jericó, Ana Bujaldón, Antonio Lamela, Hugo Mañero, Michael Daniel, Vicky Good, Louay Mikdashi, Phillip Kerr, Hubert Rampersad, Federico Moccia, Benedetta Poletti, Beatriz Ojeda, Jerome Boesch, David Trodden, Francis O'Dea, Kaisha Raeburn, Jody Ordioni, Susan Musich, Ed Cohen, Giovanni Manchia, Hussein Balaghi, Daniel Balaghi, Rowena Morais, Folayemi Olaitan, Tamara Vázquez, Adolfo Guindulaín, Simon Dray, Alysson Dray, Marta Del Pino, Isabel Manjarres, Begoña Merino, Ana Lorenzo, Ton Dobbe, Eduardo Sicilia, Plácido Fajardo, Ignacio Mazo, Carlos Espinosa, Aránzazu Montes, Jorge Cagigas, Eugenio de Andrés, Juan Pablo Ventosa, Javier Martín de la Fuente, Carlos Sánchez, Carmen Sanz Chacón, Sara Navarro, Toñín Llorente, Maite Piera, Luis Vives, Celia Gutiérrez, Esteve Montanyà, Ignacio Villoch, Consuelo León, María Prats, Pedro Gato, Inmaculada Jorge, Gastón Labadie, Ximena Fernández, Cecilia Bello, Montserrat Llairó, Cesar Villalba, Elisa Setién, José Noguera, Ernesto Manrique, Marisol Ruz, María del Mar Santana, Teresa Niubó, Francisco Cabello, Francisco Reyes, Pablo Sarabia, Teresa García-Milà, Esteve Almirall, José Navarro, Marina Romeo, Jordi Escartín, Montserrat Yepes, Olga Pons, Carme Isanta, Antonio Naz, José Morejón, Francesc Díaz, Francesc Ventura, Jorge Escobar,

Josep Manel Ventosa, Dolores Sierra, Elena Amat, Fernando Rasche, Alfonso Lorente, Giorgia Miotto, Inés Berkemeyer, Gloria Escalante, Luciano Ambra, Iván Ganchegui, Javier Estellés, Fernando Estellés, Javier Benito, Antonio Fernández-Galiano, Blanca Fernández-Galiano, Juan Carlos Marín, Juan Antonio Sagardoy, Ana Isabel Pereda, Montse Mateos, Tino Fernández, Santiago Iñiguez, Mario Garcés, Eurico Campano, Xavier Horcajo, Jesús Román, Mónica Irquiola, Pepa, Fernando Ogara, Manuel Gil, Josep Bastús, Lucia Palacios, Jesús Araque, Antonio Conde, Jeane Day, Chris Launay, Maite Sáenz, Moisés Rodriguez, Luis Oliván, Marcos Urarte, Maribel Bofill, Francisco José Pérez, Munia Cherrad, Patricia Miño, Teria Yabar, Sulaika Fernández, Josef Ajram, Mario Alonso Puig, Pol Navarro, Serafín Martín, Vicente Feltrer, Jorge Homs, Kunio Suzuki, Adolfo Moreno, María Millán, Carlos Galán.

Thank you very much

Foreword

Beware, this book will most probably change your future in a positive and powerful way!

For decades, men both wise and experienced have announced that critical talent is becoming scarcer by the day. Identifying the right talents, recruiting them, developing and rewarding them, while retaining the best ones has been a challenge that deserves all our attention. And yet, many companies and HR departments treat recruitment as a modular process that is not part of a talent strategy that ensures the execution of the business goals of the organization.

Trends indicate that the competition for talent is not over but just about to start. BabyBoomers are retiring, new generations with different preferences are joining the workplace and markets have grown more complex, unpredictable and dynamic than ever. Mobility and technology are changing today's talent game.

Thanks to recent technological developments and the use of collaborative tools, apps and the "always on" internet, the way we work and choose what company to work for and who to work with has changed dramatically. This has impacted both job-seekers and organizations looking for bright talent to realize their goals and objectives.

Amparo's work has inspired me above all by her pragmatic approach when it comes to the main HR challenges of tomorrow. She provides practical solutions that will help every reader in applying best practices to lead the way when it comes to attracting and developing key talents. Her well researched book deserves its place on the shelf of every HR professional as well as any job-seeker.

Talent 3.0 also proves that our environment is changing at a pace that is beyond our imagination. When Amparo wrote the book *El talento está en la red*, in 2011, she rightfully thought that attracting talent through social networks was a theme worth documenting, both as a guide for HR managers and recruitment officers, and for those seeking a new job.

However, five years later, newer and more relevant information abounds so the author has gathered and included it in this new edition. In this book she puts forward the concepts and techniques described in the previous book, but adds the most recent technologies and developments used to secure a talent match.

The book is primarily written for everyone who is directly or indirectly involved in recruitment and talent attraction. At the same time, it helps job-seekers to adopt the right strategy for achieving at new challenge in the fastest and most effective way.

Wim Focquet
Academic Director, Master in HR and Talent Development,
IE Business School.

Introduction

He who arrives first at the battlefield and awaits the arrival
of the enemy will be fresh for the fight; he who arrives
second at the battlefield and must hurry to be ready
for the battle will arrive exhausted.

Sun Tzu

In a context of recession and national and global economic crisis, the period between 2008 and 2016 is turning out to be one of the most difficult most business people can remember, particularly for human resources and talent management departments, which have now been cast as playing second fiddle to labour relations departments.

Despite the current economic situation, certain hints of recovery are detectable and there are indications that we are approaching a real war to attract talent and hold on to it, which gives the appearance of an actual battle to the finish.

The next expansion period in the economic cycle will mean that businesses will have to grow, and payrolls will be forced to expand. This gives rise to the question of what are and will be the most effective approaches to recruiting and how we must enter this battle fully armed and prepared to attract the best candidates. In this new scenario the use of the internet as a battlefield will play a crucial role if we intend to be more dynamic, efficient and wish to reach out to the best candidates.

From the point of view of attracting talent in business, there are a large number of companies and professionals who have set out to explore this particular battlefield:

In the U.S., 93% of recruitment strategy is based on 2.0.

Almost 46% of the world's population has access to the internet in 2016.

Social media continues to grow apace around the world too, with active user accounts now amounting to roughly 31% of the world's population.

Research conducted by GlobalWebIndex suggests that the average social media user spends 2 hours and 25 minutes per day using social networks and microblogs, with Argentine and Filipino users registering the most, at more than 4 hours per day.

Seventy percent of the companies use social media and 90% of these companies said that they benefitted from their use.

Given this evidence of exponential growth, it is easy to state that 2017 will be the year of the consolidation of 2.0 recruitment worldwide and in the following years we will see the consolidation of 3.0 recruitment. Organisations are becoming more proactive in attracting candidates from the 2.0 Web, both actively and passively, as with the supply of references in the future.

The key to success in hiring personnel using social networks lies in perfectly aligning and integrating the existing recruiting processes in the company with the technology provided for human resources departments.

Social networks and Big Data thus become an ideal way to bring businesses and potential candidates together.

1

The Evolution of HR and Talent Management 3.0.

1. Key elements in the process of attracting and selecting talent

Generation gaps: Baby Boomers, Generation X, Generation Y, Generation Z

> *Understanding personalities and managing differences*
> *and diversity are the keys to profit.*
> Álex Rovira

To understand and appropriately use social networks in the selection of personnel, it is necessary to factor in the existence of the generation gaps that exist in organisations.

When we speak of generations in the context of managing diversity, we should take into account the fact that these generations exist as groups which, while they share various features, may also be very different. In this light, for example, along with the so-called Neither-Nor Generation (the generation of young people who neither work nor study), we also have another group of young people with high levels of academic qualifications and a positive attitude toward professional development.

It should also be borne in mind that it is also impossible to compare generations in different countries because of the various histories and culture, which means that they cannot be dealt with in the same way.

Nowadays we can observe a range of generations within the same organisation - the Baby Boomers, Generation X and Generation Y (and in some cases, Generation Z which is now 17 years of age).

Generational diversity means the mingling together within a single organisation of people of different ages, skills, values, ideas, aptitudes, ways and forms of communication and consequently it also means that they are at different stages of technological development.

Chronologically we can separate them as follows:

Baby Boomers (1945 - 1963)

Generation X (1964 - 1981)

Generation Y (1982 - 1990)

Generation Z (1991 - 2010)

We can divide them up according to their history and values.

Baby Boomers

People who belong to the Baby Boomer Generation were born between 1945 and 1963, after World War II. Their dominant characteristics are: discipline, order and respect for others.

Discipline also reveals other positive qualities, such as work and stamina. They created and lived through profound social changes, including the hippie movement and feminism.

They tend to be stable in the employment world, and many of them will have remained with the same company or sector all of their working lives and are unwilling to change.

The important feature governing this group when it comes to look for work will be its serious attitude preferring fulltime work and displaying low levels of absenteeism.

These people prefer hierarchical organisations. A bigger office and a good car are status symbols and in many cases they are measurements of success depending on how fate has treated them.

A factor which should be taken into consideration regarding the Baby Boomers and their progressive adaptation to social networks is the outcome of the survey known as the Pew Internet and American Life Project which was carried out in May 2010: in the U.S., the use of social networks by internet users older than 50 has doubled over the past year, rising from 22% to 42%.

Generation X

Members of Generation X were born between 1964 and 1981, the children of the last traditionalists and the Baby Boomers. This is a generation that has observed the effects of globalisation. It grew up in a world that was already digital round the clock: mobile telephones, cable TV and the internet. Their homes have moved from black-and-white TV to the iPad.

They are breaking with the traditional patterns, including the creation of informal working environments and transforming hierarchical corporate structures into more flexible, horizontal entities.

They are loyal to their employers and they know the value of commitment.

A key value of Generation X is the achievement of a balance between professional goals and quality of life: reconciling family life with work.

Generation Y

Members of Generation Y were born between 1982 and 1993 during the technological era. They are also known as "digital natives" (a term coined by Mark Prensky), since they were born in a digital environment (as compared with "digital immigrants").

This is the first generation of young people that has grown up in an environment of collaboration and interactivity and with all modern conveniences.

Their beliefs are very different from those of Generation X; they believe that freedom of expression is more important than self-control. They are unable to exist in poverty. Even if they are not rich, it is important for them to have an easy life, simply because they grew up surrounded by comfort.

Because of this attitude to life they tend to be completely indifferent to job security. They have no fear of change and can change their jobs quickly, as they are not loyal to their employers, unlike Generation X. They prefer immediacy. What looks like a lack of loyalty in Generation Y is replaced by the value that they attach to their relationships with their workmates and supervisors.

They are also dubbed "multitasking", since they are quite capable of uploading a YouTube video while chatting on a mobile phone and tweeting at the same time.

Young people in Generation Y upload and share their experiences on Facebook and almost all would like to work for Google. This is due, among other things, to the fact that companies like Google and Facebook were founded by people in their twenties who shaped their Talent Attraction and Retention strategies by adapting them to Generation Y.

The majority of the Baby Boomers, however, have a certain hesitation, and are unwilling to launch themselves on social networks, sharing their professional lives with the world.

The biggest problem in the world is not getting people to accept new ideas, but persuading them to forget the old ones.

John Maynard Keynes

It is important to bear in mind the fact that at the present moment it is the Baby Boomers who occupy the managerial positions, along with some members of Generation X. They have always cultivated their own social networks from close proximity, based on face-to-face personal relationships or the telephone, and they have adapted to the use of email, but some Baby Boomers are unwilling to adapt to the use of social networks for selecting talent.

It's easier to shatter an atom than a prejudice.

Albert Einstein

However, it is not possible to generalise here, because some Baby Boomers have joined social networks and are using them with great success, since they are taking advantage of synergies: the advantages offered by new technologies together with their professional careers and reputation make a perfect match for new business opportunities.

For Generation Y, all social communication takes place on the net, although they don't see it as the greatest tool ever invented by man, simply because it has always been there for them.

They are quite capable of building up large communities on social networks without knowing anybody personally.

Generation Z

The members of Generation Z were born between 1991 and 2010. All their lives they have had internet access, mobile phones, MP3 players and the iPod. These are the youngsters in the modern world aged between 16 and 19, and they are also known as "digital natives".

Generation Z are super-social networkers, maturing faster than any previous generation.

They are the most entrepreneurial generation because 72% of Gen Z wants to start their own business; and they look for instant gratification.

Organisations that would like to be sustainable and last over time will have to deal with a diverse human capital. Diversity has a direct impact on creativity, innovation, efficiency and sustainability in a global and changing world, and will provide the talent which will be indispensable in the years to come.

According to the Global Webindex report (2015), some statistics of Generation Z (teens) are:

- 68% of teens are accessing the internet via mobiles, with 23% doing the same via tablets.

- 65% of teens say they spend more than an hour on the mobile internet each day.

- Facebook is still the leading app for teens (48%), although Snapchat is the fastest growing.

- Around three quarters of teens say that they spend time gaming each day – with nearly 30% playing for an hour or more.

At a global level, teens account for 6.49% of the internet population, which corresponds to an audience size of 102.89 million.

The countries with the highest proportions of online teens are South Korea and Mexico (10%). At the other end of the spectrum, teens ages 16-19 make up fewer than 4% of the online population in Canada, Singapore, Russia and Spain.

In terms of audience size, however, the importance of China is clear; it has some 33.38 million online teens. Following behind are the U.S. and India, markets that contain 12.97 and 10.24 million respectively.

Generations Y and Z, and a proportion of Generation X, are the people who most value and make most use of social networks in the context in which they live, and they have grown up with the new technologies.

What should organisations offer to attract and retain Generation Y members?

Demographic data shows that in the next few years there will be a talent shortfall and that Generation Y will predominate in organisations.

Fifty percent of the world's population are under 30 years of age. In other words, they belong to Generation Y and Z, and 96% of Generation Y uses social networks.

The top 10 characteristics Generation Y candidates look for in organizations:

1. Innovation, modernity and comfort in the working environment and opportunities to boost social relationships.

2. Opportunities for training and development. New challenges. Multidisciplinary work, because they are

young and prefer to do a variety of jobs at the same time (multitasking).

3. Collaboration with work teams, projects and joint decision-making.

4. A leadership style, which guides, participates and inspires.

5. Open communication: approachable/accessible supervisors who show a genuine interest in their professional growth.

6. Continuous feedback and output reviews.

7. A salary policy based on objectives achieved.

8. Constant access to corporate information: internet, employee portal, blogs, etc.

9. Job flexibility (cyber-commuting, flexitime, etc).

10. Organisation reputation/image or employer branding.

According to a study by Robert Half International entitled *What Motivates the Workers of the New Millennium: How to Attract and Retain Generation Y Employees,* Generation Y values opportunities to develop and the company's reputation/ brand recognition more than their job title.

The application of traditional schemes in the workplace tends to be a complete disaster for Generation Y, leading to a high turnover rate and problems in attracting and recruiting talent. Millennials also have a stronger preference for using social learning and mobile technology for improving leadership skills than other generations, and they tend to learn from others more frequently.

Managers should understand that the different perspectives of this new generation are an opportunity to find competitive advantages.

To be effective, you must pass by the right place at the
correct time, in the appropriate numbers. This is the art
of effective action in harmony with the milieu.

Sun Tzu

Many people think that talent is a matter of luck,
but few realise that luck is a matter of talent.

Jacinto Benavente

Here are some examples of human resources policies designed to attract talent, adapted to the new Generation Y:

- Cisco: use of employee referrals leads to some of the best hires for Cisco. When you refer someone, you help the company expand and diversify our network of high-potential talent. And you could earn a monetary award.

- eBay: has a meditation room for workers.

- Google: allows its employees to devote a certain period of time within their working day to projects that are not associated with the day-to-day job, and also allows them to bring pets to the workplace. It has a laundry and a relaxation room where staff can play videogames, etc. These advantages and the Google culture are transmitted to its own employees via social networks to attract talent.

- Henkel: to attract young graduates in the marketing field, it has designed *Henkel Challenge,* a marketing competition in which different teams of students design increasingly innovative products to meet the needs of consumers up to the year 2050.The winning team is rewarded with a study trip and the three best teams win an interview with Henkel's CEO and chance of an internship or even a permanent job in the organisation.

- Procter & Gamble: has set up a mentoring programme for Generation Y. Procter & Gamble has employed seniors to act as mentors for the new employees, and they in turn act as mentors for the veterans. They have managed to invert their mentoring programmes, which is a great innovation.

- Bombardier Aerospace: invited more than 33,000 employees to see the first flight of their C-Series Jet. They set up more than 45 different viewing stations in 10 countries. It was an outstanding moment. They also launched a referral program to find the best talent through their own team.

Recent surveys revealed that both Gen Y and Gen Z expect organizations to be socially responsible and to make a positive contribution to their communities.

According to Nielsen's 2014 study, Millennials are 57% more likely to interact with companies they regard as authentic and transparent. Job seekers want to work in an organization that feels real, genuine and communicative.

According to social listening tool Glassdoor, 84% of job seekers would change jobs for a company with a better reputation; conversely, 69% wouldn't take a job with a company with a bad reputation, even if they were unemployed.

The cost of not adapting to the new Generation Y will be very high: finding yourself lacking in talent in the upcoming years.

There is only one road leading to success: adapt to the new generations by making use of social networks to attract and recruit them.

Coaching versus Mentoring

Continuing with Generation Y, they ask for constant feedback and support from managers and mentors. This is an opportunity to build a talent pool in the organizations, but what are the main differences between Coaching and Mentoring?

According to the Harvard Business School, there are key differences between Coaching and Mentoring:

	Coaching	Mentoring
Key Goals	• Correct inappropiate behaviour. • Improve performance. • Impart new skills.	• Support and guide personal growth of protégé.
Initiative for Mentoring	• Coach directed.	• Protégé in charge of learning.
Volunteerism	• Employee's support is essential if coaching is to be effective; but not mandatory.	• Both mentor and protégé participate as volunteers.
Focus	• Learning opportunities. • Immediate problems.	• Long term personal career development.
Roles	• Coach to provide continuous feedback.	• Mentor to provide continuous listening. • Mentor to make suggestions and connections.
Duration	• Usually short term. • Can be "as needed".	• Long term.
Relationship	• Coach is employee's direct supervisor.	• Mentor is seldom protégé's direct supervisor.

Source: Harvard Business School.

Employer branding

If you were not already involved in this company,
would you decide to join it now?

We shall have to redefine the concept of the employer organisation
and its management in such a way that they both satisfy the legal
owners (as shareholders) and the owners of the human capital
which endows the company with its power to generate
wealth (in other words, the workers).

Peter Drucker

Trust is a key element in the creation of a company reputation, and as a direct result, of its value to the shareholders.

Robert Eckert (CEO, Mattel)

Employer branding, or in-house branding, is the process of creating identity and image management in its role as a provider of employment, and is not only based on the company's hiring strategies, but also includes a holistic focus.

The relationship between the company's values, systems, policies and forms of behaviour to achieve its corporate objectives by means of its human capital must be all factored in and managed. Companies are complex and open systems: this means that one-off actions are not enough.

Employer branding must be in step with what the company transmits to the employees, customers, shareholders and general public.

Companies must make a sincere effort to encourage the employees to adopt its mission and its values. When a company succeeds in this, it must then implement measures to maintain it. For example, when a company takes part in workplace environment studies, such as Great Place to Work, and scores well, it is a powerful recommendation for that business. You must be very wary and avoid participating in surveys of this kind if you know the results will be negative, because poor results will damage the image of the company as an employer.

An organization known in the market as a "best company" gains valuable external recognition. Beyond mere publicity, being top ranked is an important guidepost for investors, customers, and prospective candidates.

The leaders of an organisation should know what their corporate values are and communicate them to all levels of the organisation. Good leaders will find it easy to make the right decisions when they know which of the company's values and theirs are represented.

Businesses are going through a difficult time at the moment, but those who take care of their greatest asset, their human capital, will succeed and prevail in the end.

Managers who put the interests of their teams over those of individuals will encourage the commitment of their teams, and as a result productivity will increase.

Teams need transparency, and organisations must communicate, communicate and keep on communicating. From this standpoint, social networks are helping to create transparent environments.

The employees of an organisation at a time of uncertainty want only to know that someone in the company is thinking about them. All the workers will get better results if their efforts are genuinely appreciated. Fortunately, the world is changing again. We are reinventing values which we should never have lost or forgotten.

It is no easy task predicting how things will fare in the next few years, but we shall find no difficulty in guessing what will happen to those companies which have let themselves slip: they will witness a flight of talent from their organisations.

Now is the best time to act, because by then it will be too late.

When the sun comes out again and employees are leaving those businesses which failed to realise their importance in times of uncertainty, they will pay much more dearly than they would have if the measures they took had been strategic and not obsessed with the short term.

According to the "Employer branding" survey conducted by Jobvite:

- 32% of companies admit they don't have a clear employment brand strategy, but they're "working on it".

- 35% of companies do have a clear strategy; they still think it needs further development to be truly effective.

Here's a look at seven of the top employment brand "sins" companies commit today:

Mistakes	Solutions
1. You tend to "embellish" things.	• Start with what you know. • Tell a consistent story. • Communicate on platforms where people feel most "at home".
2. You're short-sighted.	• Keep a big-picture perspective based on clear standards. • Be flexible. • Metrics are key.
3. You sweat the small stuff.	• Reframe the question. • Think visually. • Show high-impact details with emotional resonance.
4. You target qualifications instead of people.	• Know the culture fit requirements for your company. • Go where the people are. • Start culture discussions.
5. You mistake clichés for core values.	• Dig deep for the specifics of your company's beliefs. • Do frequent check-ins.
6. You fail on social media.	• Being involved on social media isn't a "one and done" activity. • Give people a fun way to interact with your brand. • Get automated.

Mistakes	Solutions
7. You don't follow through.	• Be sure you have a killer career site. • Reinforce brand messages throughout the recruiting and hiring process. • Don't stop communicating your brand once employees are hired.

Source: http://www.jobvite.com

According to the LinkedIn survey "Global Recruiting Trends":

• 56% of global talent leaders say employer brand is a top priority for their company.

• 4 years is the average length of time an employee stays at one company, according to LinkedIn data.

The war for talent is biting and, as Accenture's latest survey of CEOs shows, 60% of them are lying awake at night worrying about the need to attract and retain the best people.

We are going to get the future we have created for ourselves and built. What else did we expect?

> It's no use saying 'We're doing everything we can';
> you must do what is necessary.
> Winston S. Churchill.

To create a successful Employer Value Proposition (EVP), companies must consider the following:

1. The present: potential and current employee's values and their perceptions of their organization.

2. The future: values that the organisation is trying to portray, including corporate CEO messages.

Social networks are turning into a trend and a great opportunity for the strategy involved with the creation of the brand, or employer branding.

Social networks applied to employer branding will help attract talent to the organisations. In order to succeed, the new creation of brand 2.0 will need:

- Human cooperation.

- Agility.

- The ability to constantly reinvent itself (it may well be that what worked in the past is no longer working in the present).

Recruiting becoming more like marketing could change the recruiting industry in the next years. We can build from Human Resources Areas a strong Employer Branding Plan by attending to some metrics that we use for Marketing Plans:

Marketing	Recruiting
Segment	Determine the types of people that fit your jobs.
Target	Prioritize and pursue high priority candidates.
Position	Create a narrative and message that amplifies your company's talent brand.
Product	The job and work environment.
Price	Employee salary and benefits.
Promotion	Outbound: Job postings, public relations. Inbound: Build relationships with talent communities, social, digital, and content marketing.
Place of distribution	Job boards, social and professional networks, email.

Employees who identify with their company and are committed to it will act as its ambassadors on the social networks and will be able to boost the company's corporate reputation as an employment provider.

Sixty percent of employees would like help from employers to share relevant content.

In light of the above, it is advisable for human resources professionals publishing job offers to redirect them to their corporate website where candidates can see in detail the company's services/products, its values and employer benefits.

They should also show in their "Jobs" or "Work with us" section the social networks in which the company has a presence, so that the potential candidate can access the latest updates on employment opportunities. Companies must use existing social networks to attract and retain talent.

We empower our employees to be Brand evangelists through our comprehensive social media training program. We help build our external brand by giving employees the tools and guidelines they need to communicate on behalf of the company. It's a lot of work, but the payoff is huge.

Brent Amundson, Dell

Our inclusive culture promotes a creative, innovative, and collaborative environment that helps fuel our globalization strategy.

John Chambers, Chairman and CEO Cisco

Here is an example of 2.0 employer branding aimed at attracting talent:

- Heineken: has come up with an interesting way to find the right talent for its job offer. Heineken needed to hire an intern for its Event & Sponsorship Marketing team to prepare for the Champions League final. Heineken received a staggering 1,734 applications for this position. Called "The Candidate", the video shows different interview clips of potential candidates. The video was uploaded on YouTube and millions of people watched it.

Heineken's recruitment campaign was very successful not only in the recruitment process but also in branding. Many advertising experts said that this was a very brilliant campaign, which promoted the fame of Heineken brand around the world.

Employer branding and corporate reputation have always been an important factor for businesses, but they have gained more traction with the crisis, and this is fortunately clearly reflected in company turnover.

As businesses tend to become more service-orientated, employer branding grows in importance. In a labour market as competitive as today's, employer branding, or the perceptions of employees and potential candidates, which amounts to the same thing, is as important as the way the brand is seen by a customer or potential customer (external branding), when it comes to those businesses' ability to continue to operate competitively. We should never forget that the employees of an organisation are the front-line product consultants for the brand, particularly for companies in the service sector.

Some companies are already hiring talent who specialise in this area, a new field of specialisation in the area of human resources.

The young, Generation Y, are changing the rules of the game from the bottom up, but the general management of the organisation must provide the mechanisms necessary for this inevitable organisational transformation to be exploited with maximum benefits for both company and employees.

According to the U.S. Bureau of Labor Statistics: in 2016, 50% of the population will be composed of Millennials (born after 1980) who were raised playing video games and surfing the internet to get information.

A recent survey indicated that Gen Y employees expect their jobs to be social and fun, with clear goals to succeed, and to provide personal satisfaction. They want regular feedback on their work. Gen Y is redefining the modern workplace.

Gamification creates new methods to reach out to the specific requirements of Gen Y employees.

> *The real difficulty lies not in developing new ideas*
> *but in escaping from the old ones.*
>
> John Maynard Keynes

Business Games

> *I am always doing that which I cannot do,*
> *in order that I may learn how to do it.*
>
> Pablo Picasso

Business Games can be an excellent HR tool to be used to attract talent. Some companies have been able to make the most of the opportunities offered by the internet to attract the youngest candidates; while others are ignoring this selection instrument.

Advantages of Business Games and Virtual Campus 2.0. for the company:

1. Promote the image of the company as an employer (employer branding).

2. Increase and improve the data base curriculum.

3. Increase the effectiveness of the publication of vacancies.

4. Filter the most suitable candidates to participate in the face-to-face recruitment process.

5. Valuable insights and information for staffing executives, revealing candidates who may have the job skills that traditional credentialing or sourcing often miss.

Vanessa Soames, Head of Graduate, Recruitment and Recruitment Marketing at KPMG says: "Using gamification in our recruitment marketing and attraction strategy is part of our commitment to attracting great candidates in a new and exciting way. And with the dedication we've seen from applicants/gamers so far, it's obvious we have some brilliant candidates and that the bar has been set high."

Michael Schrage, a research fellow at MIT Sloan School's Center for Digital Business, and author of the boo "Serious Play" (HBR Press) says:

"Warren Buffett and Bill Gates are famous for their love of and prowess in bridge. Harvard has used high-stakes poker as a real-world game theory laboratory for strategic thinking. For sheer bonhomie and bonding, golf remains a global opportunity for American, Asian, and European executives to mix business with pleasure. Depending on the industry, a sharp MBA who's a scratch golfer may well have a leg up in a job interview or sales meeting.

"Demonstrable talent and success at games that mix competitive fire with social skills make a desirable human capital combination. There's a perceived correlation between real competence in serious games and business effectiveness."

Gartner identified four principal means of driving engagement, using gamification:

1. Accelerated feedback cycles: In the real world, feedback loops are slow (e.g., annual performance appraisals) with long periods between milestones. Gamification increases the velocity of feedback loops to maintain engagement.

2. Clear goals and rules of play: In the real world, where goals are fuzzy and rules selectively applied, gamification provides clear goals and well-defined rules of play to ensure players feel empowered to achieve goals.

3. A compelling narrative: While real-world activities are rarely compelling, gamification builds a narrative that engages players to participate and achieve the goals of the activity.

4. Tasks that are challenging but achievable: While there is no shortage of challenges in the real world, they tend to be large and long-term. Gamification provides many short-term, achievable goals to maintain engagement.

Some examples of Business Games in Human Capital areas:

- **BBVA**: This entity bank has a virtual campus that presents the following features that adapt to new generations of talent:

  - Available 24/7: it is a permanent campus, which is available 24 hours a day, 7 days a week, 365 days a year.

  - Accessible and transparent: it is an open virtual campus, where you can navigate without prior registration. No geographical limitations.

  - Glocal: a unique recruitment portal for all units and provides details of both the group and each of their societies.

  - Interactive: a portal that allows the candidate to maintain communication directly with the departments of recruitment, which may answer their questions through an online forum and / or Downloadable channel which each unit can turn on its stand.

- Interconnected: linked to social networks using the viral effect and enabling candidates to share content networks like Facebook, Twitter or LinkedIn.

- **L'Oréal:** L'Oreal has a business game for their international recruitment strategy called Brandstorm by L'Oréal. This is a revolutionary interactive virtual platform that adapts to Generation Y, allowing students worldwide to assess and explore their career choices.

- **PWC**: PWC has released Quest, a virtual platform where contestants, from the Spanish speaking world, in teams of four, have had to do an exercise of introspection and soak up the PwC spirit.

This virtual environment is divided into three phases. In the first (Know yourself) participants take a test to know more about themselves as possible candidates in a leading company like PwC. The second phase (about us) is the resolution of 13 enigmas that requires diving into all the information that PwC has on its website. The last phase (case study) is to create a branding campaign to sell the firm in the university community. The six best works will be the finalists who will participate in one workday, this time face to face. This environment is accompanied by other actions 2.0 that allow an improvement in the flow of communication between all participants: a group on Facebook, messaging on the platform of the game, tweets, etc.

- **U.K.'s Department for Work and Pensions:** They created an innovation game called Idea Street to decentralize innovation and generate ideas from its 120,000 people across the organization. Idea Street is a social collaboration platform with the addition of game mechanics, including points, leader boards and a "buzz index". Within the first 18 months, Idea Street had approximately 4,500 users and had generated 1,400 ideas, 63 of which went on to be implemented.

- **Department of Tourism of the Australian state of Queensland:** If we put the words "the best job in the world" into Google, thousands of hits will be flagged from an excellent 2.0 marketing campaign by the Department of Tourism of the Australian state of Queensland. The aim was to promote Hamilton Island, the Great Barrier Reef and the tropical beaches of Queensland by making sure that the communications media of the entire world would publish the news.

The strategy was to organise a world-wide competition, offering a single job which they called "the best job in the world": the candidate chosen would simply be a tourist on a paradise island for six months on a salary of 90,000 euros. The only requirements to apply for this new job offer were an ability to swim and dive, a willingness to meet new people, to take photos and videos of your travels and to talk about your experiences on the internet. The winner was a certain Ben Southall, 34 years of age, who was chosen from 35,000 candidates from around the world. This is a nice example of aligning the marketing area with the human resources area making excellent use of 2.0 tools.

- **Department of Tourism of Flanders region:** In 2010 they were looking for an Erasmus correspondent for 1,000 euros per month. University students who were planning to take an Erasmus-arrangement course in the year 2011 could do so free of charge in Flanders if they were selected. In return for 1,000 euros a month, the student had to write a blog with text, images, photographs and audio recordings of the Flanders region.

Companies that want to attract and select talent must reinvent and adapt to new technologies and social networks. They should increase their efforts to attract and develop talent because future employees will be multidisciplinary, diverse, creative and involved people. This requires, more and more, polyvalent candidates capable of facing challenges in different departments and countries. In this environment, the candidate may be anywhere in the world. We must be able to reach them and social networks are an option, because this living and dynamic environment is forcing us to permanently change with it.

The evolution of recruitment methods

Until the mid 'nineties the major recruitment systems worldwide were paper-based: newspapers, universities, CVs received by companies directly mailed by candidates, temporary employment agencies, consultancies and employment agencies, etc. More recently, with the arrival of the internet, employment websites began to appear. Some of them were general in nature, in other words, offering all kinds of work, while others were vertical and specialised.

With the arrival of Web 2.0 and social networks, the employment websites have seen their business dwindle. This clearly reveals that the classical employment sites are no longer as valued as they were formerly.

Even so, the employment websites are still the market leaders, although they are battling to increase their market share, and in order to achieve this they are changing into a professional social network. Some examples of these changes in employment websites are the following:

http://www.careers.org

http://www.careerbuilder.com

http://www.efinancialcareers.com

https://www.eurojobs.com

http://www.flexjobs.com

http://www.glassdoor.com

http://www.globalhumancapitalgroup.com

http://www.gulftalent.com

http://www.healthcarejobsite.com

http://www.indeed.com

http://www.monster.com

http://www.simplyhired.com

http://www.techcareers.com

http://www.resumark.com

http://www.theladders.com

https://www.upwork.com

The situation now is that companies are using social networks to recruit talent and the fact that the employment websites' control of the sector is threatened has caused them to change and adapt to social networks.

At a global level, the professional social network with the greatest number of users is LinkedIn, although Xing and Viadeo are also popular. The professional social networks offer companies a selection of the best qualified employees, and are ideal for seeking highly specialised, highly trained professional profiles, while the employment website labour exchanges offer a service which is more quantitatively and generically focussed. In the face of this new reality, companies and candidates will have to design different strategies for themselves to find talent and employment respectively.

In today's 24/7 communication environment, the keys for HR success are based in a dynamically networked world.

Reinvention does not consist of changing what already exists, but of creating what does not. Some organisations reinvent themselves in their supply and demand planning and in the way they attract talent. They are creating a future youth pool focused on Generations Y and Z, which will take its place in their organisations in the future.

Talent hub

A talent hub is a location that contains a critical mass of talent with the skills and expertise required by employers in a specific company, industry, or collection of industries. The creation of a talent hub may be driven by "demand" or "supply" (for example, higher education or oversupply of labour due to industry diversification).

For example, in order for Walmart to successfully expand into Brazil, one of the fastest-growing economies in the developing world, it has had to collaborate with government and academia to develop talent with the critical retail skills it needs.

Saudi Aramco, for instance, has had to actively develop the engineering and technical talent it needs to effectively manage the country's vast oil reserves.

This is a HR vision that embraces the talent innovations of today and makes a proactive commitment to developing tomorrow's workforce.

The economic global trends are shaping the Human Capital world:

— Talent globalization

— Market volatility

— Changing employee expectations

— Technology landscape

The evolution of HR activities

According to the *Harvard Business Review*, HR activities closely track the labour market:

- Early 1990s: The HR function (known as "Industrial and labour realtions") was born. After steel and oil had transformed U.S. business in the 19th century, it became clear that workforce management needed its own discipline

- 1920s: In a thriving economy, good workers were hard to come by and even harder to keep. HR induced supervisors to treat people well.

- 1930s: During the Great Depression, supervisors favoured the "drive" system of management (threatening and sometimes hitting) and saw HR as a hindrance. Workers put up with almost anything to stay employed. Talent development was practically non-existent.

- 1950s: After World War II, one third of the executives died in office with no one to replace them. To fill that void, HR created a host of revolutionary hiring and development programs.

- 1970s: As the economy slowed, labour was once again plentiful. Business leaders started undoing all those post war programs designed to attract and develop talent.

- 1980s: The U.S. went into a deep recession, and workers clung to their jobs. Rather than invest in HR, companies pushed hiring and development tasks onto line managers, who had neither the time nor the training to do them properly.

- 1990s: During the dot-com boom, companies competed fiercely for "employer of choice" status to meet their soaring talent needs. So HR enjoyed a brief heyday, focusing primarily on hiring and retention

- 2001: When the doc-com bubble burst and the economy tanked, business leaders felt little urgency to attract talent. Productivity rose, wages stayed flat, and HR lost the influence it had enjoyed during the boom.

- 2016: With the effects of the Great Recession of 2008 still lingering, most people with jobs aren't jumping ship yet, so executives feel no urgent need for HR programs. HR must make a case for them.

According to the Global Leadership forecast (2015) by The Conference Board CEO Challenge:

Today, HR professionals are categorized into one of these three roles:

1. Reactor: Ensuring compliance with policies/practices; providing tools/systems when asked.

2. Partner: Openly exchanging information about current issues; collaboratively working toward mutual goals.

3. Anticipator: Using data to predict talent gaps; providing insights linking talent to business goals.

HR's role needs to continue to evolve. For at least two decades, the challenge for HR was to move from being administrators or reactors to being business partners. It's now time to raise the bar for HR, to take on a new role we call "anticipator". Anticipators are always looking for what might come next. They work with the business to predict future talent gaps, and then strive to close the gap. They are able to proactively advise leaders on the probability of their strategies based on available talent and its quality.

While anticipators and partners generally are likely to use similar leadership practices, anticipators do six things differently than partners or reactors.

Anticipators:

- Put a stronger focus on programs that foster employee creativity and innovation.

- Are more likely to position leadership development as an integrated journey rather than an independent series of events.

- Are more likely to institute negative consequences for managers who fail to develop their leaders.

- Help ensure that a higher percentage of leaders are promoted from within.

- Help leaders be more ready to meet the CEO challenge of human capital.

- Are much more likely to use advanced workforce analytics, particularly those that involve forecasting future talent needs.

The new role of HR professional 3.0

To define the role of a qualified professional to manage people, 3.0 competence should consider the following dimensions:

- Promotes and leads organizational change.

- Collaborates and works as a team with a more commercial vision develops high integrity and honesty, develops communication skills.

- Skills to deal with new technologies and Web 2.0.

- Capacity for constant learning.

- Promotes innovation and creativity in a proactive way.

- Develops his own personal brand on Web 2.0.

- Builds relationships.

- Ability to manage diversity.

We live in a world of constant change, which we must adapt to in order to survive in it.

1.2. Development of the internet and new technologies

Studies have shown that social relationships are one of the best indicators for predicting human happiness throughout the world. There is a clear correlation between social relationships and happiness.

Eduard Punset *(The Soul is in the Brain)*

Evolution of communications media: Too much information?

It was only 20 years ago that we were writing letters on typewriters, but with the birth of the internet and the "www" (World Wide Web) we began to send them by electronic mail, even adding files which contained photographs. Nowadays we might upload those photos to Facebook, share them on Instagram, Flickr or Pinterest.

In 2010, the following item was published on the website www. elpais.com, which makes us realise how much technology has changed in recent times and how it is affecting our lives:

"Belgian Olivier Vandewalle, who threw a bottle into the sea 33 years ago with a message inside received a reply 33 years later on a popular social network. At the time he was spending his holidays sailing off the English coast when he tore a page from an exercise book and decided to recount his adventure. Thirty-three years later, Lorraine Yates from England found a bottle with a message inside which was still legible in Swanage, on the south coast of England. Lorraine did not hesitate, and with the only information she had, the name and place of origin of the writer of the message, she decided to have a look on Facebook. When the Belgian read Lorraine's addition to his profile he remembered that message he had sent when he was just a teenager."

The way in which we relate to others has changed. We communicate with each other in different ways. The new technologies have meant that it is no longer necessary to be physically present in order to maintain and support personal relationships.

Since the internet has become established as a means of communication and in addition to this Web 2.0 is a growing phenomenon, we now have in our reach much more information than we are capable of processing.

> *Men cannot live if they lack forms of mutual cooperation.*
>
> Eric Fromm

Evolution of Web 1.0, Web 2.0, Web 3.0 and IoT.

The world wide web was created in 1989 by Tim Berners-Lee and Robert Cailliau.

In the early days of the internet, the Web was purely one-way, in other words the information was strictly informative and allowed for no direct interaction with and between the users.

Nowadays it has become two-way and allows for interactions of all kinds of content in real time.

Web 1.0

Web 1.0 began in the 1960s in the most basic form in existence, with text-only browsers. The next step, in the nineties, saw the appearance of HTML, which made website pages more attractive to the eye, and the first visual browsers made their appearance, such as Internet Explorer, Netscape, etc. Web 1.0 is read-only.

The user cannot interact with the content of the page (no comments, responses, etc.).

Web 2.0

The term is closely associated with Tim O'Reilly, because of the O'Reilly Media conference on Web 2.0 in 2004.

Web 2.0 is the representation of the development of traditional applications to Web applications focused on the end user and which generate collaboration. Web 2.0 is also known as the "social Web" or "people Web". The main maxim of Web 2.0 for companies is to devote time to people.

It represents a new era of collaboration since it permits its users to interact with other users or to exchange website content, in contrast with non-interactive sites (Web 1.0), where users were restricted to passively viewing the information being supplied to them.

We have passed from a static Web (Web 1.0) to a Web where two-way action, accessibility and collaboration are the outstanding elements (Web 2.0).

Web 2.0 is transforming the processes of selection It presupposes a reduction in cycles, lower recruitment costs and the possibility of reaching a larger audience thanks to freedom of publication and distribution.

We have moved on from "whom I know" to "how I reached this candidate", to the development of a strategy whereby human resources professionals and candidates in search of a new job can approach the universe of the internet.

In other words, we are in a new participatory and collaborative environment, one in which talent can be discovered in a flexible and direct way.

The 10 main characteristics of Web 2.0 with regard to attracting and selecting talent are as follows:

- Interactivity.

- Openness.

- Transparency.

- Collaborative learning.

- Multidirectional.

- Communication.

- Sharing.

- Reputation/trust.

- Fun.

- Freedom of publication and distribution.

These networks are growing at an exponential rate, producing a cultural change which is so dizzying that it has revolutionised the use of the internet and job seeking.

Advantages:

- They make it possible to establish relationships between people who share the same interests, as well as the permanent updating of contacts.

- A presence on a social network is an excellent personal branding tool since these kinds of networks see themselves as a showcase for talent.

- With regard to the employment environment, they are an excellent pathway for the active search of candidates or jobs.

Disadvantages:

- The invasion of privacy is the big problem caused by social networks. And for some countries, network membership is seen as a threat to national security. The result is that staff working in security-related jobs in these countries is not allowed to use them.

- Exposure on the internet and the digital trail creates a digital identity which, if not taken care of, can damage the personal brand or employer brand.

- Social network membership has on occasions become an addiction.

The origin of the social networks on the internet dates from 1995, when Randy Conrads created the website http://www. classmates.com. His plan was that users of this social network would be able to restore or maintain contact with old school or college friends.

However, once Facebook was created it became consolidated as the fastest growing social network.

The popularity of these platforms has grown exponentially and large companies and internet multinationals have launched new projects based on social networks.

Web 3.0

Web 3.0 is associated with a new stage that is designed to give meaning to the web. Tim Berners-Lee, the creator of the World Wide Web, also calls it Web 3.0. or the Semantic Web.

The increase in interactivity and mobility are two factors that appear to have been decisive in this new stage of the Web. Basically, the idea refers to a Web capable of interpreting and interconnecting a greater quantity of data, which will make an important step forward in the field of knowledge possible.

Designed correctly, the Semantic Web could support the development of human knowledge in its totality.

Web 3.0 has also been used to describe the developmental path taken by the internet, which leads to artificial intelligence. Content Management Systems (CMSs) and search engines are working hard to make the web more semantic.

An example of Web 3.0: Companies like IBM and Google are incorporating new technologies which will make it possible to predict which songs will be hits using university music Webs as an information base.

The Internet of Things

Even as we continue to define what Web 3.0 means, we are simultaneously moving beyond it, and toward the Internet of Things. The Internet of Things (IoT) will likely be the next era, as it takes the notion of an ever-present internet to a new level. Smart devices in the Internet of Things not only use the internet, but speak to each other via machine-to-machine communication (M2M) to accomplish tasks without the need for human input.

The theory of the six degrees of separation

There is nothing like relationships. In the entire universe, everything is related to everything else. Nothing exists in an isolated form. We cannot think of ourselves as individuals capable of creating ourselves without the help of others.

Margaret Wheatley

All social networks are based on the theory of the six degrees of separation. According to this theory, every single individual can be connected to every other person on the planet through a chain of acquaintances containing no more than five people (making a total of six connections).

The theory was originally put forward in 1929 by the Hungarian writer Frigyes Karinthy in a short novel entitled "Chains". The concept is based on the idea that the number of acquaintances grows exponentially with the number of links in the chain, and only a small number of connections are needed for the group of acquaintances to become the entire human population.

There is no stopping the growing need to be connected, to have a social life, to use technology and connectivity in support of it, and to use a range of devices for that purpose.

And the fact is that the way in which we communicate, the tools we use and the relationships we establish help us to define our digital identity, supporting our personal promotion via ever increased activity on the internet.

Marketing expert Seth Godin refers to today's economy as the "connection economy", in which value is created by the connections we make. We can say the employers now need to develop an ecosystem where job seekers and the public engage with their brand, learn about it and get the right information at the right time. This is the key to attracting and retraining the best talent.

Digital identity

The brand is everything and the perceptions people have of the brand are 90% of the brand.

Paul Kedrosky (CNBC Television)

A person's digital identity, or NETREP (Net Reputation) is the reputation which a physical person or company has on the internet.

When a human resources professional puts the name of a possible candidate into a search engine such as Google, the best thing is that this name will then appear on a dedicated website, showing that the individual is in contact with other outstanding personalities in the sector. This is one of the virtues of possessing that professional digital identity.

At the present time our digital personality is an aspect of our identity, a complementary part of our lives. Not possessing a digital identity, that is, not appearing on social networks, is beginning to be seen as being unknown, as lacking transparency as far as candidates are concerned.

The trend is to reveal yourself on the internet as you are in your everyday life, and from the professional point of view this is essential, since this is the only way to generate trust and find work, do business with a potential client, be contacted by a headhunter, and so on.

From the point of view of the business, having checked on your brand reputation on Google, you should then design a strategy to improve it, to discover who you are, where you are and what is the behaviour of the people who talk about your reputation and brand on the internet.

Glassdoor http://www.glassdoor.com is a website which shows the salary statistics of thousands of companies, mainly in the U.S., together with the most common questions asked of candidates by human resources professionals. It includes statistics drawn from the information supplied by the users themselves, who flesh out this website with opinions, evaluations, etc.

According to Charles Fombrun, president of Reputation Institute, the study assessed the dimension whereby a company builds its reputation: the quality of the products or services it offers, innovation, leadership, working environment, integrity, financial results.

Companies should have a community manager who will monitor the opinions of the company expressed in social networks and act appropriately. As we have stated before, employer branding must be established and maintained.

Below we have listed some of the 2.0 tools that are useful for monitoring information and corporate or personal reputations on social media:

Addictomatic, Alltop, BackTweets, Blogsearch, Board Reader, Booshaka, Delicious, IceRocket, GoogleAlerts, Google News, Google Trends, GoogleVideos, ItsTrending, Keotag, Syomos, SocialMention, Technorati, Trendistic, Tweetag, TweetReach, Twellow, Twitter Search, WhosTalkin, and Yahoo! News.

The Pareto Principle and Mind maps

The Pareto Principle says that 20% of an action produces 80% of the effects, while the remaining 80% is responsible for only 20% of the effects.

One of the best-known practical applications of this principle is to be found in the analysis of sales or commercial actions. Companies that carry out a turnover analysis regarding customer numbers observe that approximately 80% of turnover depends on 20% of the customers. The exact 80-20 relationship is, of course, almost never observed, but the ratio between sales and customer numbers is usually in that region. Using this information it is possible to decide which customers are strategic (and must be looked after) and which have less impact on the profit and loss statement. In the case of Twitter users, for example, statistics confirm that it complies with the Pareto Principle: 20% of Twitter users generate 80% of the total tweets. In general, thanks to the Pareto Principle, it is possible to analyse a situation and make strategic decisions working with real data (for example, by making use of the networks which best suit our personal/corporate goals).

To improve the way we organise our time, and to optimise the new tasks which we must deal with in both our professional and personal lives, we can make use of what are known as "Mind maps", the procedure defined as mind mapping.

"Mind maps" are a semantic representational diagram used to represent ideas and definitions related to a central concept or project.

Their main feature is that they are very graphic and visual, thanks to their structure in the form of a network. The flood of ideas we may have are thus organised around a central concept and are reflected in a document which we can revise from time to time to add notes, use colours to emphasise priorities, activities, jobs to be done, and so on. In this context we can mention a free-of-charge 2.0 too that will help us design "Mind maps": XMind. Also worthy of note are the following: Mind Genius Business, MindManager, Mindmeister or Mindview Business.

The Johari Window

The Johari Window is a model invented by two U.S. psychologists, Joseph Luft and Harry Ingham, in which they define the information about the self that a person is aware of in the mind. Johari is just a word invented by the creators of this theory that is made up of the first letters of their names.

The Johari Window model is based on the supposition that an individual can increase his knowledge of himself by means of interpersonal communication with those around him, maintaining the two-way flow of information (a characteristic of Web 2.0 communication).

A study of different professional profiles can reveal different levels of openness of the Johari Window. A marketing professional, for example, will reveal a higher level of openness of his upper window than other profiles.

What we have here is a model that attempts to explain the flow of information from two viewpoints:

– "Self", feedback: how and to what extent we know ourselves (how much is accepted from others).

– "Others", the exposition: how and to what extent we expose ourselves to others (how we are revealed to others).

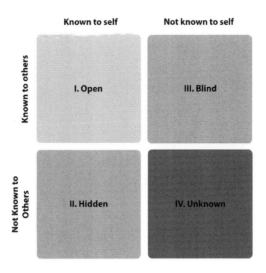

The four panels in this window:

- I Open panel: what I know about myself and also what the rest of the world knows about me.

- II Hidden panel: what I know about myself but which I do not share with others or that increasingly undervalued phenomenon, which is privacy.

- III Blind panel: what everybody else sees in us and which we are unaware of (the impression we have on others).

- IV Unknown panel: what neither we, nor the others, are aware of (the unconscious).

From this point of view, social networks and new 2.0 technologies tend to reduce zone II, because they support communication.

We should take care to bear this model in mind when interacting with social networks so as not to commit communication errors.

2

New Technologies in International Talent Search

The men who have changed the universe have not achieved it by manipulating the leaders, but by mobilising the masses. Manipulating the managers is the method of intrigue and leads only to secondary results. But manipulating the masses is the sign of the genius who changes the face of the world.

Napoleon Bonaparte

Human resources professionals are increasingly turning to the potential offered by new technologies in the processes of selection and making use of social networks in particular to attract Generation Y, members of which nowadays make up the young energy of the labour market and who are completely familiar with the use of new technologies, as well as other profiles with specific technical or middle management content.

The companies that have adapted to social networks are provided with recruiters who open corporate profiles on Facebook, public job calls and offers on Twitter, and seek candidates on professional networks such as LinkedIn.

At the same time, selection processes using videoconference and/or teleconference interviews via Skype or instant messenger and even psycho-technical testing and other aptitude tests on line are increasingly common.

From the point of view of the candidates, the internet is already yet one more way to find work. Not only do they post their CVs on employment websites, but they also keep their profiles updated on the networks and send retweets of the job offers they see on Twitter.

Below we have included the main icons associated with new technologies and used in the area of human resources, especially in attracting and selecting talent.

2.1. Categories of social networks: generalist, professional, vertical

We can adopt the following as a classification:

- Generalist: Facebook, Google+, etc.
- Professional: Linkedln, Xing, Viadeo, etc.
- Vertical or specialised: Esanum, Innocentive, Moterus, etc.
- Others: Twitter, Blogs. YouTube, Instagram, Flickr, Pinterest, etc.

2.2. Features of social media in the talent search process: SMS, WhatsApp, Wikipedia, Google, Skype, YouTube, Twitter, Facebook, Google+ LinkedIn, Xing, Viadeo, Delicious, Instagram, Flickr, Pinterest, WordPress, Blogger, Slideshare, RSS, Bit-ly, Hootsuite

What do these icons mean? What practical application do they have in Recruitment 2.0?

SMS · WhatsApp · Wikipedia · Google · Skype · Youtube · Twitter · Facebook · Google+ · Linkedin · Xing · Viadeo · Delicious · Instagram · Flickr · Pinterest · Wordpress · Blogger · Slideshare · RSS · Bit-ly · Hootsuite

SMS

Some companies send an SMS to candidates to confirm with them the date and place of their employment interview and to wish them luck. Apart from being an excellent communication medium on the cost-saving front, the personalised message wishing the candidate luck contributes added value to the employer branding strategy to attract talent.

Recently people are using the messaging service WhatsApp which has more than 500 million users worldwide.

WhatsApp

Some companies that have direct contact with candidates use this chat app. The use is more common when you need to contact a final candidate for the recruitment process and the candidate is located outside your country. You can use the call option offered by WhatsApp and you can save the cost of a regular phone call. Within China, WeChat is the dominant force; it is used by 84% of the mobile audience, giving it a user base of nearly 325 million in that market alone. It also does well in a number of other APAC countries, including Hong Kong (42%), Malaysia (38%) and India (21%).

Outside of China, WhatsApp has now overtaken Facebook's own Messenger service to become the top global chat app – being used by nearly 40% of the mobile internet audience each month. Following behind Facebook's services are Skype (32%), Viber (12%) and Line (10%). The rest of the apps tracked in the chart are used by relatively small percentages globally, although this can mask strong uptake among certain demographics or in particular markets.

Wikipedia

Wikipedia is an encyclopaedia in which the information is supplied by internet users themselves. *Wiki* is a Hawaiian term that means quick. Using Wikipedia, candidates can check the information of the company to which they are applying (history, press notes, share value, etc.) and in this way be better prepared to face a selection interview. In any case, the corporate website of each company should be the first place the candidate checks to obtain more information about the company.

In their book *Wikinomics,* Don Tapscott and Anthony Williams have this to say:

"A new art and a new science of collaboration are emerging, and we have dubbed it Wikinomy. The new science of Wikinomy is based on four powerful new ideas: openness, interaction between equals, sharing and global action. These new principles are replacing some of the older precepts of the economy".

Google

In 1998 two young Stanford University students founded Google and it is now the search engine most used by internet users.

Human resources professionals use Google to obtain more information about the candidate. In some cases, when a company has checked the candidate's name on Google it may decide not to contact him. This shows the great importance of a person's digital identity, the personal branding which every professional will keep on the internet. Likewise, candidates must check all the relevant information about a company in Google before applying for a job and before the job interview.

Skype

Some organisations use this communications medium to save costs on in-house calls between staff members in the same company and also to carry out selection interviews with candidates who reside in other countries.

This internet call service allows up to five people to take part simultaneously in a videoconference.

YouTube

Three young men working for PayPal − Jawed Karim, Chad Hurley and Steve Chen − created a website which they called YouTube. It was bought by Google in November 2006.

In the narrowest sense, YouTube cannot be considered a social network, since it does not lead to interaction between its users, but it has become one of the reference icons of the social web. Its most common use in the field of human resources is to publish corporate videos to attract talent and for employer branding strategy.

Companies in different sectors have already posted videos on YouTube (lasting between 2 and 5 minutes) to attract talent. The videos communicate the corporate values of the respective organisations and the advantages they offer their employees. This means that it is an excellent employer branding strategy medium.

In this way companies can communicate their corporate values to potential candidates in a more transparent way and reach millions via Web 2.0.

Twitter

As microblogging or nanoblogging networks we can mention Twitter. In the strictest sense, these types of networks cannot be considered social networks because they do not cause interaction between their users.

These types of networks base their service on the constant updating of user profiles by means of short text messages, which do not exceed 140 characters.

This means that it is possible to make available information that is clear, concise, simple and fast to all the other users about activities which are taking place at that moment, such as impressions, thoughts, publications.

All updates are shown on the webpage of the user profile, at the same time as they instantly appear on the following pages of other users.

Facebook, Google+

Facebook: It is a general social network that was created in 2003 by Mark Zuckerberg in his Harvard bedroom. This is currently the social network with the most users worldwide. Facebook is used by some companies to publish job offers and provides for the inclusion of an "I like it" button on a website or blog. This is the button all Facebook users use when they see a job offer they like and they would like to share with their contacts. It is then published on the news panel of their Facebook friends. This small service has a great deal of potential regarding the content (it is yet another way in which a job offer can reach a large number of potential candidates).

Google+: It is a general social network that was created in 2011.

Google+ tends to take second place in fast-emerging internet markets. These are the countries that use Google + as a second social network: Argentina, Brazil, France, India, Italy, Malaysia, Mexico, Poland, Philippines, South Africa, Spain, Taiwan, Thailand, Turkey, UAE and Vietnam.

LinkedIn, Xing, Viadeo

These three are the international professional social networks which are most used by human resources professionals to recruit talent.

The information that appears on these networks is updated by the user and even includes recommendations from former colleagues, supervisors and providers, which facilitate the search for information on the part of human resources professionals.

The cost savings in the selection procedure is really significant, since they provide a real showcase of talent. Contact can be made directly with the candidate and direct communication then maintained.

LinkedIn: Founded in 2003 by Reid Hoffman, LinkedIn connects the world's professionals to make them more productive and successful. With over 300 million members worldwide, LinkedIn is the world's largest professional network. In June 2016, Microsoft Corp. snapped up LinkedIn Corp. for $26.2 billion in the largest acquisition in its history, betting the professional social network can rev up the tech titan's software offerings despite recent struggles by both companies.

Xing: The professional social network Xing bought out the largest professional platforms in the Spanish-speaking world: Neurona and eConozco. It has a significant presence in Germany (its country of origin), Spain and China.

For processes in Germany, Xing is the network with the best results, particularly when we are looking for a professional of German origin, for both top and middle management positions.

Viadeo: It has over 50 million users worldwide. It is a social network with a low penetration in France, given its French-speaking origin. For this reason, it is recommendable for human resources professionals who wish to attract candidates who speak French or who are residents in France.

Delicious

This is a social bookmark which makes it possible to retain and share links with various websites in a single location and to classify them by category (labels or tags): business, candidate, news related to the sector, the company, competitors, bulletins or newsletters.

Before the appearance of Delicious, when you found a website you liked, you included it in the favourites on your internet browser.

In this way human resources professionals can organise blogs, employment websites or web pages that they use frequently, keep the links or news about a sector in which they are interested in a more accessible way, and arrange them using a labelling or tagging system.

Not only can you store websites, you can also share them with other Delicious users and find out how many have a given link stored in their bookmarks.

Instagram, Flickr and Pinterest

Instagram, Flickr and Pinterest are websites for storing and exchanging photographs on the social web. Some companies use this social network to display photographs of corporate events, conferences, employment fairs, and the like.

Wordpress and Blogger

WordPress and Blogger are free blogs.

Companies are able to access the candidates' blogs and check, for example, the level of knowledge they may have on a subject and the way they think. In this way, the human resources professional will be in possession of more information leading to a more exhaustive understanding of the candidate's profile.

Slideshare

This application makes it possible to upload and share presentations. For example, we can use to publish corporate presentations, press releases, etc

RSS

Businesses use this tool to offer candidates who, for example, would like to join a company access to the latest published job offers. This saves multiple visits to a variety of websites to check on the updated content.

Using RSS (Really Simple Syndication), candidates and companies can register for those websites which may be of interest to them and read the content without having to visit them. RSS can subscribe using applications allowing these sections to be read. An example of an RSS reader is Feedly. Feedly can be used to see on a single page all the updates of the internet pages in which we are interested, (free) registration with the various RSSs, such as employment websites, specialist blogs or the financial press, the latest job offers published on a website with which the reader is registered, the latest entry on a blog, the latest news published in a financial newspaper, and so on.

Employment websites are now designed with an RSS. This streamlines candidates' job seeking, since, if the candidate is looking for work as an accountant in London and is registered with the RSS for this check, when a new job offer is published on the website, the candidate will know about it at the same moment without having to visit the web page. In recent years websites have been designed so that a search can be maintained, and updates will be sent to you by email, but now with the RSSs, these checks are updated on the content aggregator or headline reader with which the user is registered and the user does not have to check through hundreds of emails in his inbox.

RSSs make job seeking easier for the candidate from the point of view of flexibility, since he can be the first to see the offer and send in his CV.

RSS news readers are excellent tools whereby we can quickly and easily access the latest publications on our favourite websites.

Bit.ly
http://www.bit.ly

Bit.ly is an internet address shortener.

Many social services such as Twitter and their clients only allow you to write a certain number of characters (in the case of Twitter, just 140 characters), which is why this application is very useful.

If we had to shorten addresses by hand, the process would be as follows:

1. Enter the Bit.ly website.

2. Enter the address we wish to shorten in the appropriate field.

3. Click the "Shorten" button.

Also you can see how often users click the shorten link and then you can monitor the number of impacts and from which countries they click. It is very useful to measure the ROI in Recruitment as you can see how many users click on a job offer and compare it with how many CV's you receive.

Hootsuite

This is a platform which speeds up interactions with social networks. It makes it possible to manage a number of accounts and identities, to create a personalised view for labels and searches, to see trending topics, to programme messages to be sent when we wish, to follow users and to add them to the lists, to share photographs, to shorten URLs, and to download traffic statistics graphs, etc.

It is very useful for obtaining quantitative data regarding tweet numbers, the increase in followers, etc.

Clients include: Harvard, Dell, Economist, NBA and Walt Disney.

2.3. LinkedIn

These are seen as the best support tools for establishing professional contacts with other users.

Registering and creating a profile on LinkedIn

Registration is simply a matter of following the instructions as they appear on

http://www.linkedin.com.

Some LinkedIn users place the word LION or premium next to the title of their profession. What is the meaning of LION on LinkedIn? LION is the acronym for LinkedIn Open Networkers. These are users who do not restrict invitations, who accept all users who send invitations to them. And what is a premium user (shown with the initials IN) on LinkedIn? This is a user who pays a subscription to LinkedIn to enjoy the following significant advantages:

1. Advanced search: through this a greater number of results (and candidates) can be obtained.

2. Organiser/agenda: which allows the user to organise contacts in flexible fashion (similar to labels) and not just first grade contacts, but all contacts.

3. Receive invitations/messages from any user on the internet (even though they may not be connected to the user's network) without them having to be premium (which makes for a greater change of increasing contacts).

It is important to point out that most users allow their contacts to see their own contacts. On occasions there will be users who prefer to opt for privacy as regards their contacts, meaning that their contacts cannot see the contacts that the user has, which may possibly give rise to some level of suspicion, and in most cases will end up with your being eliminated as a contact, when it becomes apparent that you have nothing to offer. However, these profiles will usually be those of headhunters, who are adopting this approach for reasons of client confidentiality, etc.

It is advisable to have a profile that allows your contacts, the contacts upon which you depend, to be viewed. There are many examples of company managers and executive officers whose contacts are open, because it is understood that you invite/accept trustworthy individuals or people where the contact has been via third parties among your contacts.

Communicating and creating a network of contacts on LinkedIn

Once the user has registered, communications via LinkedIn can be via:

• Invitations.

• Messages.

• Presentations.

• Inmails (emails whereby the user pays a premium for the service).

The LinkedIn applications also allow contacts to be imported from Yahoo.com, MSN Hotmail and Gmail email accounts, among others.

The following can also be added manually:

• Contacts (the contact's email is entered directly).

• Workmates (LinkedIn suggests those in the companies where you have worked).

- Fellow students (LinkedIn suggests those who took the same courses as you).

Recommendations on LinkedIn

It is very useful for professionals in search of a new position to ask for recommendations from their former work colleagues, suppliers and supervisors. This will help them to be valued more highly on social networks.

For headhunters and selection chiefs it is very useful to have this information available on the spot without having to make telephone calls, etc. The time and cost savings are significant.

Main advantages of professional social networks

From the point of view of the professional who is looking for a job or wanting to change his job:

1. They make it easier to look for new employment opportunities.

2. They facilitate the establishment of new professional contacts or promotion in the workplace.

3. Users come into contact with other professionals in their field via shared trusted acquaintances, which helps improve connections with others who, in normal circumstances, would be inaccessible because of the nature of their position or responsibility.

4. Their usefulness depends on the user keeping his profile up to date and active.

From the point of view of an employer to attract and recruit talent:

1. They help to identify possible "talent showcase" candidates who could be involved in their selection processes.

2. They make it possible to obtain more detail regarding the information available on the profile of the candidates selected in a given hiring process.

3. They open the possibility of launching a network of contacts with a greater degree of specialisation.

4. Their users have a medium or high professional profile and executive positions abound.

LinkedIn is beyond a doubt the professional network with the greatest penetration worldwide and has the clear objective of being the professional social network par excellence. This being the case, we shall spend a little more time going into some detail on those of its features that are of interest in Attracting and Selecting Talent, as well as job seeking.

Most common uses in attracting talent:

- Advanced and selective candidate search (sector, speciality, etc.).

- Creating and sharing interest groups.

- Publishing job offers.

- Extending the network of professional contacts.

- Creating and/or improving employer branding.

Direct search for a candidate in LinkedIn

From the upper toolbar of the main menu the human resources professional should enter the keyword for looking for the position he wishes to fill in his organisation (engineer, for example).

A search can also be made using the name of the target company (this technique is very commonly used by headhunters who are going in search of a candidate according to his previous experience in specific companies or in a specific sector). The names of everybody who works or has worked for that company will be displayed.

It is also possible to use the system to undertake advanced searches in order to improve the results.

Advanced searches can be made with keywords, names, surnames, company, etc.

The search results will show the people with various degrees of separation.

Level 1. Direct contacts from our network.

Level 2. Contacts with one degree of separation.

Level 3. Contacts with two degrees of separation, and so on.

We can contact our first level connections directly by a message.

The remainder of the indirect connections we can add to our network of contacts or request a presentation to one of our first level contacts.

How can a candidate find a job offer on LinkedIn?

There are three ways:

- Jobs on LinkedIn (on the upper browser, the advanced job Search tab).

- Group search (the candidate must be a member of a group to see those offers which are offered in the groups).

- Direct search in companies (on the upper browser, first and second level companies appear on the Companies tab, and next to them whether they have published job offers on LinkedIn is shown).

How does a company publish a job offer on LinkedIn?

There are two publication options:

OPTION 1 (paid)

Access to this zone is via the upper bar of the main menu, in the "Jobs" section, in the job offers publication area.

The publication will remain on the internet for 30 days.

Advantages: it reaches 400 million of the top professionals worldwide. Job offers published on LinkedIn receive an average of over 100 candidates.

OPTION 2 (free of charge). Publication of the job offer in an interest group.

Procedure:

1. From the main menu, go to the "Groups" section. Publication is free; although some groups will require prior approval by the administrator, and others even prohibit job offers.

2. Once we have detected the group which is of interest to publish a job offer and we are members of that group: go to the group employment tab and publish the vacancy. It is advisable for vacancies that are published to have some relationship with the content of the group. Indicate the keywords of the sector or the discipline of the group desired and put down the details of the description of the

job offer. Candidates who are members of the groups can answer directly in a private message to the human resources professional who published the offer.

For example: El talento está en la red / Talent 3.0. (the professional LinkedIn group of this book with nearly 10,000 users), among others.

How do you create a group on LinkedIn?

On the top bar of the menu, click on "Groups" and follow the instructions, indicating:

- The name of the group.

- Enter the logo.

- Choose the type of group and put in a brief description of it.

Leveraging LinkedIn tools including APIs and Groups is a great shortcut to drive relevancy and interaction. To download free "Follow" buttons and the Company Insider widget, go to developer.linkedin.com/plugins.

How do you become a member of a group on LinkedIn?

LinkedIn allows you to be a member of a maximum of 50 groups. Some groups have subgroups, but they are not counted in the maximum total of 50 groups per user.

It is for this reason that it is crucial to apply the Pareto 80/20 Principle, in other words, you should be a member of those groups which have a large number of members or specific sectors/interests and which help us to achieve our objectives.

If we undertake a search by group subject area they will be displayed in order of largest to smallest according to the number of members.

Candidates looking for a new job can undertake a group search for the words human resources/Headhunter/Staffing & Recruiting. When they perform this search, all the headhunters who are in groups should emerge, and since you share groups with them, you can send them a direct message. The majority will show their email address on the same profile.

Candidates are advised to join interest groups and participate with their opinions so that in this way they will contribute an added value, attracting the headhunters who will read their comments as experts in the field.

It is worth reminding jobseeker candidates of the acronym of the mythical AIDA modem (attraction, interest, desire, action).

Some human resources professionals use interest groups on LinkedIn to publish job offers at no cost in a segmented form. These groups make it possible to reach a target which coincides with the sector and operational area of the offer, and stimulating a high quality response.

However, some groups require the prior approval of the administrator, and other groups prohibit this, or have disabled the employment area.

According to Jan Vermeiren, author of best-seller *How to Really Use LinkedIn and Let's Connect*, it is important for companies to create a corporate group on LinkedIn, since it can increase the value of the number of members and attract more members in a variety of ways:

1. A presence on the LinkedIn network together with corporate events will help members to keep in touch between meetings.

2. User members of the corporate group who find it difficult to attend many meetings can continue to be connected via the group.

3. The LinkedIn group is a platform which helps the other users to analyse the trends in the sector.

4. Some potential members would never have heard of your organisation if they had not seen your group on LinkedIn. In this way, they will be able to contact the company by first having made contact with the corporate group and becoming a new member of your organisation.

5. It is an effective and free alternative to creating a forum on your own website. Many organisations find it difficult to build a successful community, since they lack a critical mass of people to take part in the discussions. As a result people don't visit the forum, the negative spiral continues and the outcome is that almost no one visits the website. Given the fact that people use LinkedIn to connect up with others and to build their network with people other than the members of their organisation, they will continue to use LinkedIn and from time to time they will visit the group of the organisation created on LinkedIn.

How do you find a company group on LinkedIn?

On the upper browser, on the Groups tab click on "Groups search", stating the name of the company.

Company example CISCO:

The first group to appear allows access to CISCO employees, suppliers, etc.

In any case, CISCO has created different groups on LinkedIn: Cisco related groups such as Cisco Professionals, Cisco Certifications.

The profile of a LinkedIn company

On the upper browser, choose the Companies tab and click on "Company Search" to reveal the companies of the first and second level contacts. It is also possible to see those who have published a job offer on LinkedIn.

How does a company add to, or personalise, its profile?

The LinkedIn team is working towards a goal whereby very soon companies will be able to modify certain information in the profile of their company, such as the description, the address of the head office, the website and the turnover. They will also be able to:

- Post entries intended for jobs.

- Post recruitment videos.

- Upload images of the company.

- Include other promotional material for recruiting.

How can you see information on a LinkedIn company?

We can display the data which may be useful to us for selecting talent:

- Company data.

- Employees currently working there.

- Statistics regarding the history of these employees in the company. This information is very interesting for headhunters who are interested in discovering the companies in the sector where they can find candidates for another company, etc.

There is another LinkedIn button, "Follow us on LinkedIn", which companies can add to their corporate pages and link them to LinkedIn. In this way, companies can increase the traffic on their websites and create more links with their potential candidates. In regards to potential candidates, with "Follow us on LinkedIn" they can receive updates such as the most recent offers of employment which are published on this professional social network.

2.4. Facebook

The most common use of Facebook by human resources professionals

- To publish job postings on the company´s wall Fan Page or specialised group.

- To seek information of a personal nature about the candidate (hobbies, lifestyle, etc.) which they would not ask in a personal interview. This factor has given rise to an interesting debate as to whether this action is a breach of the right to privacy or not. What we can say is that if a candidate publishes certain information in a transparent format in his Facebook profile for all internet users, then it is understood that companies can inspect that profile.

This yet again underlines the importance for candidates of being extremely careful with personal and professional information that they display on social networks.

It is essential to explore the various levels of privacy offered by each social network and each service.

It is also not advisable for candidates to mix professional and personal contacts in the same group, as inconvenient information could cross over. For example, Facebook allows the creation of groups with different levels of privacy and access to comments, photographs, videos, etc.

Facebook offers a wide range of applications and features which allow users to dispose of external communication tools by providing them with a platform which incorporates all the necessary applications on the same screen in which they can organise and arrange various aspects of their everyday lives.

Although Facebook is a general social network and not a professional social network that specialises in job seeking, the fact is that some companies use it for Attracting and Selecting Talent for the following main reasons:

1. It is able to reach over 1.600 million registered users (potential candidates) at the world level.

2. It is possible to see more detailed information about the candidate (information which is not shown on the CV).

3. It improves the employer brand for the purpose of attracting and retaining talent. It helps raise the loyalty of potential candidates and employees.

4. It establishes a direct channel of communication with potential candidates via which companies can find out what is thought of them.

5. It establishes a meeting place between the employees and staff members of a company, with the possibility that this can be a private communication channel.

6. It communicates corporate information of interest to potential candidates: employee benefits, job offers, links to the corporate website/corporate videos.

7. It provides a pool of fans (potential candidates) in the future for the company.

8. It facilitates the organisation of corporate events or webinars to attract potential candidates.

How to create a Facebook Careers Page

When a Facebook page is being created, it is important to place it on the search engines and ensure that users get real value from it, as this will in turn generate more fans (potential candidates):

1. The name: it is important to choose the name carefully, whether it is the name of a product or service. When the user reaches a total of 25 fans he can personalise the URL of the page from facebook.com/username.

2. Invitations: inviting contacts from other social networks via Twitter or email in a first instance. Invitations must continue to be sent via other communications media: email, on the email signature, on the company business cards, and so on.

3. Create lists: this is a speedy way to accumulate fans on Facebook. The lists must be separated according to classification, for example, employees, potential candidates, etc. Lists can be created sharing events, news, suggesting the page to other contacts, etc.

4. The "About Us" section" describes the company including keywords and the URL of the corporate website.

5. Information tab: includes the most relevant keywords, the URL of the corporate website and describes the company in greater detail.

6. Use applications: to improve the user's experience on the page so that he spends more time there. The use of Twitter from Facebook is also advisable, as this will attract more fans to Facebook.

7. Use the widget with the "I like it" button on the corporate website, jobs section.

8. Add links on the wall: links to an external website (an external corporate website) can by published on the wall, producing a viral effect. By default, the fans of a Facebook page are always going to see the wall as an opening page. In order to attract potential candidates or fans the profile must be attractive. Here we should recall the acronym of the mythical AIDA model (Attraction, Interest, Desire, Action).

9. Update content: this should be done on a daily basis, or at least every other day. It is important to answer all comments and eliminate spam-type publications.

For example: Ernst & Young US Careers has a page on Facebook https://www.facebook.com/eyuscareers with around 140,000 fans and on which candidates interact with the company. Ernst & Young employees also exchange experiences, etc. They have defined two separate channels for recruiting talent via Facebook: one for candidates with experience, and another for new graduate candidates. They also have a photographs page of admirers where users exchange photographs related to the firm. It is an excellent strategy for employer branding.

Some examples of Facebook fan pages:

http://www.facebook.com/AllianzCareers

http://www.facebook.com/ATTCareers

http://www.facebook.com/BoeingCareers

https://www.facebook.com/eyuscareers

http://www.facebook.com/MicrosoftCareers

http://www.facebook.com/tacobell.careers

http://www.facebook.com/UnileverCareers

http://www.facebook.com/UN.Careers

http://www.facebook.com/walmartcareers

In business communications, Facebook is a network which is used a great deal to promote its services/products and to attract talent to its organisations.

2.5. Microblogging networks: Twitter

Most common uses in attracting and selecting talent

- Creating lists.

- Sending corporate website links.

- Extending the network of professional contacts.

- Publishing job offers free of charge.

The phenomenon of these types of networks is seen, for example, in the following:

- The English version of the Collins dictionary has been expanded with new words among which we note Twitter and to tweet;

- Griffith University in Australia has introduced the subject Twitter in the study plan for their degree in Journalism.

According to the public relations bureau Burson-Marsteller, the language most used on Twitter is English (61%). One of the uses of Twitter is to connect to and recommend corporate videos, and according to a study referred to on Mashable, it is the social network which shows more reference videos, with a difference of 28% compared with 6% on Facebook. One of the reasons for this is the facility and speed of use of Twitter.

Twitter is very effective as a method for directing traffic to corporate websites, employment portals and for improving presence on search engines such as Google.

In just a few seconds, you can recommend a video to your followers. The study shows that people who visit the video will spend more time watching it than as a result of any other form of recommendation.

Twitter possesses some key concepts which are very useful for attracting and retaining talent: following someone, searching for someone, tweeting, retweeting, hashtag, direct messages, creating lists, etc.

What does following someone on Twitter mean?

Following someone means receiving updates from the person/company which a user is following on his own record.

The statistics list of followers/followed appears on the profile of the user, and if you are a follower of someone, they can send you private messages, also known as direct messages.

Following someone is not an application for friendship, as on other social networks. Unlike other social networks, following someone on Twitter is not mutual.

How do you search for someone on Twitter?

Twitter allows you to find users by means of keywords, places, interests, job offers, what the network thinks of a company, etc.

On the navigation bar at the foot of the page is a useful tool: "Twitter Search".

By entering any word, results can be obtained in real time. For example, you would like to know what users are saying about a company. We run a search for the keyword "company".

You're wondering who's tweeting in your zone. Search by place, "city name", to see a list of the users in that city.

What is tweeting?

Tweeting means sending a tweet or 140-character message via Twitter.

Job seeking candidates as well as human resources professionals are advised to write their tweets with 100 or 115 characters so that this will allow other users sending a retweet to add their comments without having to shorten the tweet (the best known shortener is bit.ly).

Candidates seeking a new job or company employees who use Twitter must be careful when sending a tweet and must be aware of the fact that these can be monitored by their boss or potential headhunters, which means that before sending a tweet the candidate must realise that he is creating his digital identity and leaving a digital fingerprint.

What is a retweet?

When a user sends a tweet and this is tweeted again, it is referred to as a retweet (or tweeting another tweet).

Enrica Tomasina, selection manager for Yahoo! EMEA, says:

"Recently, our human resources colleagues at Yahoo! Brazil had to hire some technical staff for their offices and they asked us for help in Europe (Yahoo! EMEA).

"Via the Twitter followers we have at Yahoo! EMEA we tweeted internet links with various offers to come and work at Yahoo! Brazil. From the Yahoo! Brazil human resources area we were able to reassure ourselves as to the quality of the candidates (followers of the Yahoo! EMEA Twitter account) who were supposed to be of high quality, even better than if they could have been selected in situ or by means of a Brazilian selection company."

"We were also able via Twitter to interact with the candidates interested in working for Yahoo! and we selected some technical profiles."

There is an ever-growing number of job offers appearing on Twitter as well as users sending tweets offering jobs.

Not only do employment agencies and headhunters make active use of the tool to seek candidates via this channel, the companies themselves are already using it to save time and money, since publishing job offers is free of charge and a link can be made with the corporate website so that the candidate can send his CV direct to the company.

Retweeting (sending a retweet) is a new feature that helps people to share information quickly, which is precisely the purpose of Twitter. To retweet, the cursor is placed on the tweet and the retweet link is clicked. Retweeting is not only an excellent way to distribute information via Twitter, it is also an excellent way to discover new and interesting content. Twitter now shows the information of a retweet for all public tweets.

What is a hashtag?

On Twitter it is very common to see a tweet which contains the hash sign # followed by a keyword: this is a hashtag. It is used to monitor and classify tweets and to help facilitate the search for subjects or keywords. For example, if a candidate is looking for a job, he should go to "Twitter Search" and indicate the #job or #jobs.

What is sending a direct message?

On Twitter you can send a message directly to your followers, also of 140 characters. This message is only received by the user to whom it is sent.

What is creating a list?

On Twitter you can create lists of followers following a criterion for keeping the users we are following classified as well as possible. It is not advisable to create lists of a confidential nature, such as a list of the employees of a company, since this list is public and could be used by competitor companies.

Twitter accounts related to employment

Until the appearance of social networks, employment websites seemed to be the first option for recruiting talent. However, with the inclusion of social networks in the world of work, allowing for direct contact between individual and company, the situation has slowly begun to change.

Twitter has become a very important tool in business communications, but now it is not just important for the ICT sector and bloggers, who use it to distribute content, but for a variety of companies in other sectors, which now have a user account on Twitter to communicate directly with customers and potential candidates.

The following are examples of websites concerned with job seeking at the international level: @twellow, @twiting4job and @exectweets

Some companies already use Twitter to publish job offers at no cost and which reach thousands of potential candidates: @googlejobs, @StarbucksJobs, @TWDCjobs, @MicrosoftJobs, @GHCGjobs and they use the hashtag #job or #jobs

Recommendations on the use of Twitter for human resources professionals

A few recommendations for human resources professionals regarding effective use of the tools for selecting and attracting talent:

1. Always include the corporate Twitter account in all your communications, whether they are email, or whatever. The followers are potential candidates.

2. Use hashtags when sending tweets via http://www.twubs.com

3. Use the URL shortener via http://www.bit.ly.com or other tools such as, https://www.hootsuite.com

4. Use applications which allow you to speed up your tweets, for example via Hootsuite.

5. Use applications which analyse trends on Twitter via http://twitteranalyzer.com

6. Display corporate photographs to upgrade your employer branding and in-house communications.

7. Send tweets connecting corporate video links so that they reach a greater number of potential candidates, via http://www.youtube.com or http://www.vimeo.com.

8. Improve the search information on candidates.

9. Promote a corporate event to attract talent or job offers via http://vite.io

10. Involve your employees as "ambassadors" to increase the number of followers.

Regarding the following table we can see the Twitter IDs of the 50 most valuable brands according to Forbes Magazine in the U.S.:

Rank	Brand	Industry	Twitter ID
#1	Apple	Technology	@appstore
#2	Microsoft	Technology	@microsoft
#3	Google	Technology	@google
#4	Coca-Cola	Beverages	@cocacola
#5	IBM	Technology	@ibm
#6	McDonald's	Restaurants	@mcdonalds
#7	Samsung	Technology	@samsungmobile
#8	Toyota	Automotive	@toyota
#9	General Electric	Diversified	@generalelectric
#10	Facebook	Technology	@facebook
#11	Disney	Leisure	@disney
#12	AT&T	Telecom	@att
#13	Amazon.com	Technology	@amazon
#14	Louis Vuitton	Luxury	@louisvuitton
#15	Cisco	Technology	@cisco
#16	BMW	Automotive	@bmw
#17	Oracle	Technology	@oracle
#18	NIKE	Apparel	@nike
#19	Intel	Technology	@intel
#20	Wal-Mart	Retail	@walmart
#21	Verizon	Telecom	@verizon
#22	American Express	Financial Services	@americanexpress
#23	Honda	Automotive	@honda
#24	Mercedes-Benz	Automotive	@mercedesbenz
#25	Budweiser	Alcohol	@budweiser
#26	Gillette	Consumer Packaged Goods	@gillette

Rank	Brand	Industry	Twitter ID
#27	Marlboro	Tobacco	–
#28	SAP	Technology	@sap
#29	Pepsi	Beverages	@pepsi
#30	Visa	Financial Services	@visa
#31	Nescafe	Beverages	@nescafe
#32	ESPN	Media	@espn
#33	H&M	Retail	@hm
#34	L'Oreal	Consumer Packaged Goods	@loreal
#35	Hewlett-Packard	Technology	@hp
#36	HSBC	Financial Services	@hsbc_uk
#37	Home Depot	Retail	@homedepot
#38	Frito-Lay	Consumer Packaged Goods	@fritolay
#39	Audi	Automotive	@audi
#40	UPS	Transportation	@ups
#41	Ford	Automotive	@ford
#42	Gucci	Luxury	@gucci
#43	Nestle	Consumer Packaged Goods	@nestle
#44	Accenture	Business Services	@accenture
#45	IKEA	Retail	@ikeausa
#46	Siemens	Diversified	@siemens
#47	Wells Fargo	Financial Services	@wellsfargo
#48	Fox	Media	@foxtv
#49	Pampers	Consumer Packaged Goods	@pampers
#50	Ebay	Technology	@ebay

2.6. Vertical or specialist social networks

Vertical social networks are also known as specialist social networks. Their dominant characteristic is the fact that they look for areas of specialisation, which is the key to their success. Vertical networks of very different types are steadily making their appearance, such as networks for people fascinated by cars, IT, marketing, cooking, etc.

Vertical social networks are extremely effective in the selection of talent, since, for example, a candidate in love with motorcycles will find a company on a social network devoted to that theme. Thanks to the vertical networks, companies can approach a target profile that suits their sector.

Both candidates and companies can look for the specialist networks on the internet which best suit their interests. We can always use the Google search engine, but also available are: Blog Search Google among others.

Most common uses in attracting and selecting talent

– Direct search for candidates by sector/specialisation: employers can undertake a direct talent search in the precise sector where their business operates.

More examples of vertical or specialist social networks:

• Moterus: http://www.moterus.es for professionals and lovers of the motorcycle. The HR team of Piaggio uses this social network to recruit talent.

• Innocentive: http://www.innocentive.com is a social network for professionals who specialise in developing technological networks. It has over 90,000 users. An example of a company which uses this social network is

P&G to find talent specialising in R&D. It is even possible to work for P&G without having been put on the payroll, since this company offers financial rewards for professionals with this network who take part in some specific R&D projects.

- StratosS: http://www.stratos-ad.com is a social network for developers. Here we can find a series of professional profiles specialising in the development of applications: graphic artists, musicians, programmers. On this specialist network users can participate by means of forums, chat rooms or wikis. The wiki is used a great deal on this kind of specialist network, since the same users participate with their contributions to draft specialist articles and between them all they amend the information in such a way that in the end a content which is the consensus of all the users who have participated is created and which, as always, has been approved by the administrators of the same social network.

- Raptr: http://www.raptr.com especially designed for computer game aficionados.

- Esanum: http://www.esanum.es for doctors.

- Bytepr: http://www.bytepr.com for communications professionals.

- Universia: http://www.universia.es for academics and university personnel (teachers, researchers). It advertises job offers, grants, etc.

- Discapnet: http://www.discapnet.es is the website for the disabled, where individuals with different functional possibilities can access a wide range of work positions and can register their CVs.

2.7. Blogs

Blogs have become a powerful communication tool for many companies and freelance professionals.

Many companies have made use of this 2.0 tool to raise customer loyalty, since the blog provides details of the latest news in the sector, and it attracts future candidates. It is a clear example of how synergies can be exploited in the marketing and communications fields and in company human resources sections.

Corporate bloggers for companies as big as Coca-Cola, General Electric, Microsoft, Walmart or General Motors, among others, offer Web 2.0 communications guidelines which they subscribe to in their joint blog: Blog Council. Member companies include: Kellogg's, McDonalds, Dell, P&G, Microsoft, HP, UPS, 3M, Sunguard, SAP, Walmart and Amway.

Here are some high-profile examples of corporate blogs:

- Microsoft: in the blog in which Bill Gates, founder of Microsoft, explains the latest technology news, he describes his most recent thoughts and ideas, and also recommends books he has read and which he found interesting. If a user would like to follow him, his blog has a direct link with Twitter as well as containing RSSs for subscribing to his news (http://www.gatesnotes.com).

- Acciona: it has a corporate human resources blog (http://canalempleo.acciona.es) where users can interact directly with the company. Worthy of note is the section where various members of the company staff have collaborated to record videos giving their own point of view, which is also a positive experience for the protagonists.

At the international level, the following are worthy of mention:

– Dell: http://en.community.dell.com/dell-blogs/default.aspx.

- Disney Parks: http://disneyparks.disney.go.com/blog.

- Google: http://googleblog.blogspot.com.

- O'Reilly Radar: http://radar.oreilly.com.

- Play Station: http://blog.us.playstation.com.

Below we have listed the blogs most used (free of charge): WordPress and Blogger.

WordPress and Blogger

They manage a great volume of content in different formats.

They provide mashups: they use content for other internet applications to create a completely new content.

They are ideal for social networks and professionals can create their personal brand.

According to Syomos, the distribution of blogs by country, the United State is in first place, the United Kingdom in second place, Japan number three and Spain in eighth position. But blogs are not only useful for companies; they are also used to look for jobs or to share experiences.

2.8. Tools and applications 2.0 and 3.0

Klout
http://www.klout.com

This allows you to find out the influence of a user on Web 2.0.

Here are some of the 2.0 applications that speed up the management of social networks:

Twitterfeed
http://www.twitterfeed.com

This is a tool which allows you to publish the entries from a blog on the Facebook wall and on Twitter. In this way, when a fresh entry is published in a blog (for example: WordPress or Blogger), without the user having to tweet this new post, this system automatically sends a tweet.

As an example of the use of Twitterfeed, we might mention the first digital human recourses publications: BBC, @bbcworld.

Audiense
https://audiense.com/

It is an application that allows preparing a review of our Twitter account and to know, for example, who are our more influential users, who have stopped following us, and even what times are our most active supporters.

Tweetstats
http://www.tweetstats.com

By simply entering the Twitter users, this service allows you to analyse and produce statistics regarding the number of tweets, the time when they occurred, retweets, and so on, so that you can then analyse all the information and identify trends.

Shareaholic
http://www.shareaholic.com

This is a personalisable add-on which allows you to share content with over 60 social network websites. Clicking on the Shareaholic icon, you can immediately share the website you are visiting (which automatically reduces the link for you). It also shows in real time trend themes, which allows you to view the latest news, videos and blogs.

3

Personal Branding 3.0. The Professional Profile of a Candidate and Job Seeking on Social Networks. New Professions Emerging from the 3.0 Environment

The candidate's CV or personal profile

Just as eBay is the virtual store which never closes, LinkedIn is the 24/7 employment showcase.

Juanma Roca

The CV you put on LinkedIn is 10 times as effective as a normal CV, because using your LinkedIn profile you can make your CV, references and references available to headhunters and human resources professionals.

Dan Schawbel

Over recent decades, if a candidate wished to take part in a selection process, it was essential that he should send in his CV via the company corporate website, the employment portal in Word, PDF, etc.

The CV or personal profile should be the business card of a candidate who is looking for a new job and wishes to supply the appropriate information for attracting the attention of the human resources professional.

The majority of human resources experts in the field of selecting and attracting talent are in agreement that, depending on the importance of the position or profile, the time a human resources expert should spend reading a CV should be not less than 30 seconds and not more than five minutes. Within that period the CV is either accepted or rejected. It will be rejected for two simple reasons: lack of precision on the part of the candidate or because the candidate does not match the desired profile of the job, and lacks the presence, weight or importance required to do it.

When they fail to find a potential candidate on LinkedIn, some headhunters also tend to discard candidates on the assumption that they have not adapted to the new technologies.

Key elements in a professional profile: personal branding

The best way to achieve a good reputation is to succeed in being what you seem to be.

Socrates

Whatever our age, our position or the business in which we work, we must all understand the importance of having a brand. We are the managing directors of our own business: Me, Ltd. In order to operate in today's marketplace, our most important job is to take responsibility for marketing the brand called You.

Tom Peters

Real personal branding is a journey to a happier, more successful life. Your personal brand should always reflect your true character and should be built on your values, strengths, unique features and virtues.

Hubert Rampersad

In a CV or professional profile, personal branding is crucial.

According to Dan Schawbel, personal branding expert, author of *Me 2.0: Build a Powerful Brand to Achieve Career Success,* the three main characteristics of a brand are:

1. Transparency.

2. Authenticity.

3. Credibility.

These are Dan Schawbel's 10 recommendations for creating a 2.0 brand:

1. Become an indispensable asset for both work colleagues and customers within the contacts network.

2. Position yourself as the right person to be approached, and hence to contact.

3. Gain confidence in yourself.

4. Focus on social value, not cash value.

5. Build up a list of contacts before you need to contact them.

6. Extend and publicise that personal brand in a range of forums.

7. Become so recognised that even people who don't know you can talk about you.

8. Make that brand so visible that no one can forget it and no one can avoid it.

9. Be a creator or producer of content, not just a consumer of content.

10. Keep an open mind, and one which is focused on generating a broad network of connections.

Meg Giuseppi, on the other hand, has her own 10 recommendations for creating a 2.0 brand:

1. Google yourself, in other words, look for yourself on Google.

2. Put your own name on Google alerts so that you're advised about anything that comes up on the internet about you.

3. Buy the domain myname.com.

4. Create an identity mark or your own symbol for emails, the post, etc.

5. Register with the main social networks, beginning with Facebook, LinkedIn or Twitter.

6. Start blogging.

7. Launch your own website.

8. Write book reviews for Amazon, Barnes and Noble, etc.

9. Join professional associations.

10. Share your own know-how and experience on a range of forums.

LinkedIn is the perfect showcase for boosting your personal 2.0 brand, whether from the point of view of a candidate looking for a job or that of a company which can establish its values by communicating them on the internet.

According to Hubert Rampersad, personal branding expert, author of *Your Personal Brand,* the history of a personal brand is like the "elevator pitch": a short, clear, succinct, carefully planned and well practised description of your personal brand that people should be able to understand during the time it takes to go up a few floors in a lift. Your elevator pitch speaks clearly about the qualities that make you unique and which mean you are better prepared than the others. It should be possible to say everything in two minutes, it should be attractive, stirring and should get people to know you and understand you with ease, and should make them want to spend more time with you.

What is "Googling yourself"?

Everybody keen on developing a professional career should Google themselves to find out what is being said about them, and to check whether they are achieving the objectives of their personal 2.0 brand. In other words, enter your name into the Google search engine and see what websites appear.

What usually happens if a person is registered with LinkedIn is that one of the first references in a search for their name on Google will be their profile on LinkedIn. Hence the importance of the fact that a candidate's profile should state their profession and/or the words which a headhunter will use to launch the search:

- Sales manager.

- Human resources manager.

- Chief executive officer.

- Chief financial officer.

- Engineer, etc.

Possessing an excellent profile on LinkedIn depends not only on your CV but also on visibility on professional social networks. For example, a candidate is interested in a specific objective, working for Coca-Cola, and uses LinkedIn performing a search on "HR Manager, Coca-Cola, and country". The result it gives will be the exact name of the person as well as the connections you share with this person.

You should then look for the mutual connections you have, and you might discover a connection with your neighbour. A candidate would not have known this, because Coca-Cola would never have brought it up in conversation. Having discovered the connection on LinkedIn, the next step would be to talk to your neighbour, who would probably agree to write an email to introduce you to the Coca-Cola HR manager.

Registering with a social network is easy, but time must be invested in the matter to attract followers, contacts or to build communities or even a good digital reputation and to create a personal 2.0 brand.

In actual fact, this is a very methodical procedure and certain rules of conduct must be observed, rules which are indeed in force, although never published, which will help us to succeed if we apply to the internet the common sense we use with the relationships we build in the real world.

According to an interview with Juanma Roca by Amy Vanderbilt, "Lots of people would prefer to remain in the same job all their lives. But the world of business is changing at a very rapid rate and that means you must be prepared to change at the rate of that change. Young people from Generations X and Y are used to making frequent changes and they usually have many more social and professional contacts via LinkedIn. But people who are not represented at all on LinkedIn and who don't use it as an extension of themselves will end up watching their career stagnate quite astonishingly."

The huge popularity of LinkedIn has turned this website into an excellent professional directory and advertising notice board with job offers.

A strong, communicative LinkedIn profile strengthens the personal brand, experience, success and exceptional value, and increases the likelihood of being contacted by a headhunter.

There is quite an art to designing the way in which we wish to be seen on the internet, with our personal and professional image, and to building an on-line reputation with suitable visibility in keeping with our goals. This means we must undertake a certain amount of self-examination to decide what is the correct strategy for us to pursue on Web 2.0.

Of course, a social network is very different from a professional network, and yet the correct use of both can be very useful from a professional point of view. We should never underestimate the power of the personal angle of social networks in professional interaction, given that, since they are based on maintaining contact with one's most proximal environment, they can act as a vehicle for employment opportunities, and a very high percentage of offers on the job market are accessed via our own personal contacts. However, networks that have become known as professional networks have turned into very specific tools for connecting up at a professional level and seeking new opportunities, since their strategy is concentrated on making our professional profiles visible in specialist forums.

Recommendations for an effective job search on LinkedIn

1	Make sure the profile is 100% complete.
2	Add a clear and concise header and a relevant profile with useful words for search engines.
3	Managing references.
4	Extending the contact network.
5	Update the profile often.
6	Take part in interest groups.
7	Set up an interest group.
8	Making use of websites on the network of your profile: Twitter and blog.

1. Make sure the profile is 100% complete.

If a human resources officer is planning to make an appointment with a candidate for an interview, he is bound to put the candidate's name into Google and in most cases this will pull up the LinkedIn profile, since this normally appears among the first five results (given the traffic and popularity of LinkedIn). So if your profile is not 100% complete, lacking in references and an updated employment record, it will not make a very sound first impression.

2. Add a clear and concise header and a relevant profile with useful words for search engines.

After the family and given names, the headline is the first thing which human resources professionals will see on the LinkedIn profile.

Just as we would do when drawing up a CV, we must be clear and concise with the header and headline of the profile. Of course, the personal brand which the candidate wishes to communicate to the potential employer is very important, which means that he must have decided beforehand on the information he wishes to publish in his profile, considering only such data that are relevant and match his experience and professional interests. To streamline the LinkedIn search engine profile search, a profile must be defined using key words, such as "technical industrial engineer", "marketing manager", and the like. This will make your profile more visible and more relevant. Consideration should also be given to the question of publicising certain parts of the profile, such as the email address, to facilitate contact data for the benefit of the human resources professionals.

3. Managing references.

A traditional CV will include a limited number of references. A candidate filling in his profile on LinkedIn, however, can include a large number of references. References from human resources professionals who personally know the candidate will help in the decision-making process, often leading to contact being made.

We can also make use of a separate application, but one which links to LinkedIn and Facebook to seek references: http://www.talentag.com.

4. Extending the contact network.

Contact should be made with work colleagues, suppliers and professionals whom you know from conferences, who have trained you, who are associated with your area of expertise and who can facilitate contact with more users. A guideline for adding connections in a consistent manner is to begin with the best known, then add people you have met in a natural way at meetings, congresses, and so on.

Some LinkedIn users believe that it is only necessary to connect with a small number of professionals whom they know and trust. Others feel you have to connect with everybody. The reality is that when a candidate is looking for a job, he can never be sure who will be able to help him. This means that when you contact users, you must always send a personal message indicating the reason why contact is being made or how the connection with that person took place, as well as asking if there is any way in which you can be useful to them. In this way, you can break down the possible initial barriers and illuminate other reasons which may appear as to why contact should be made or not. It is not advisable to send references of the "spam" variety, because some users may reject the invitation and on some occasions, if there is a repetition, LinkedIn may adopt measures, such as sending a warning message:

"NOTE: this message is to advise you that you are very near the limit for "I don't know him" responses to the invitation you have sent to various users, and having reached this point it will be necessary for you as of now to indicate the email address of the LinkedIn users every time you send invitations. Please remember that you are only supposed to invite persons whom you know."

It is also advisable to extend the contacts network before looking for a position, since some people may see this as a search for a specific interest and reject the invitation.

5. Update the profile often.

Devoting some time to our profile and keeping it up to date will help us improve our digital identity, the visibility of the profile and increase the likelihood of being contacted by a human resources professional. It is advisable to indicate in the profile whether or not the candidate is looking for work: "I am open to job offers". The best thing for a candidate who is actually looking for a job is simply to inform others that you are "actively searching". What is not recommended is to suggest in a rather informal or negative way the fact that you are out of work. For example, "unemployed, on sabbatical" - there are many ways to say the same thing, but in a positive way. Other unadvisable approaches are including the sentence: "I am unemployed" and then including four or five children on the photograph (I have also seen this case on LinkedIn, but when that individual appeared I advised against it, and the photograph in question is now more standard).

LinkedIn facilitates communication, since information updated by the users is updated and transmitted to the contacts network. For example, every time a candidate changes his profile, indicating that he is seeking "new professional opportunities", this will appear on the main page of all members of his contacts network.

6. Take part in interest groups.

Groups are an excellent way of finding a job, because they will include a section where "vacancies" are published on a regular basis. In addition, some groups include tens of thousands of human resources professionals. As a member of a group, a candidate can send a message to almost anybody who happens to be a member of the group (even though not included in their contacts network).

Membership in interest groups concerned with areas associated with the candidate's current occupation or any other which can be seen as professional offers a more complete picture of the user's personality and hence of their digital identity. It should be borne in mind that synergies are important and that small details can make all the difference when it comes to finding an interesting job.

7. Set up an interest group.

Being the founder of a group has many advantages: it allows you to send messages once a week to all the members and be seen as a thought or opinion leader, etc. This is a different way of finding a job, because it amounts to attracting potential employers or human resources heads who might be interested in a candidate. It must be said that it is very important to maintain an excellent digital reputation; otherwise the results will be the opposite of what is being sought.

8. Making use of websites on the network of your profile: Twitter and blog.

Adding your blog and Twitter is a good first step for a candidate actively seeking a job. All you have to do is connect your LinkedIn profile with your Twitter account to ensure that your tweets and posts are syndicated to LinkedIn. This saves time and makes it seem as though you are more active on LinkedIn, as well as allowing you to exhibit regular activities and experience. LinkedIn also offers a number of additional applications, such as posting PowerPoint presentations, sending notice of upcoming trips, and so on. This all helps to reinforce the professional profile on LinkedIn and make its content more attractive.

There is no need to be disappointed if results are not immediate. As many people say, "Looking for a job is a job in itself." This means that you must effectively build up your contacts network and maintain an active presence on LinkedIn. As long as a candidate remains consistent with his short-term professional objectives, new professional opportunities will arise from social networks.

The most positive aspect of this process is that when the candidate has found a job, he will have a network of contacts which he must continue to groom and extend. In this way, with a contacts network, the next time he is looking for a job, it will be much easier. We should bear in mind that in the upcoming decades jobs will not be as permanent as they were in the past.

Recommendations for an effective job search on Twitter

1	Completing de profile on Twitter in a professional way.
2	Tweeting in a professional way.
3	Following those recruiters who could be of interest.
4	Using job-search tools.
5	Activating RSS alerts.

The factors whereby a candidate stands out from the others and helps him to create a personal profile on Twitter which matches his professional goals are:

1. Completing the profile on Twitter in a professional way.

– Enter a real name and avoid names which might be unprofessional.

– Detail your professional skills (in your biography, Twitter allows you to write 160 characters).

– Use a real photograph with a professional appearance to it, as though it were for a CV. The majority of Twitter users prefer to follow users with real photographs as they generate transparency and trust.

– Use a personalised background to promote the personal brand.

– Include a link to a CV in the biography (for example, include a link to a professional profile on LinkedIn). Use a tool such as VisualCV. A candidate can establish himself on Twitter as an expert in his profession, thus supporting his know-how and experience.

2. Tweeting in a professional way.

– Watch your spelling, language and style of communication.

– Bear in mind that any human resources officer can see your profile and how you interact, and this will influence the decision as to whether to arrange an interview or not with a potential candidate.

– Increasing the number of followers as much as possible can lead a human resources head to assess the user as a potential candidate since it denotes proactivity and contributes interesting knowledge. It is important to bear in mind that tweeting repetitive content is not advisable.

– Sending thanks for retweets (abbreviated as RTs) and/or sending messages directly to the followers.

– Using the hashtag so that human resources chiefs can detect the profile they are seeking more quickly, such as #manager or #engineer.

– Avoiding turning into a spammer with the consequence of having Twitter delete the user's account.

3. Following those recruiters who could be of interest.

Many recruiters do, in fact, use Twitter to look for potential candidates. Before contacting a recruiter via Twitter, the candidate must be satisfied with the following: his biography, the number of his followers, and finally, he must seek references on the internet to find out whether the recruiter is a credible source or nor. You could, for example, use Twellow http://www.twellow.com, among others already mentioned, to find users.

4. Using job-search tools.

A reactive job search on Twitter is probably not the best way to find a job. A number of tools and applications exist to assist with the proactive job search.

Example of a job-search tool:

– @TweetMyJobs: this is a tool which arose from Twitter for candidates seeking work and also for the recruiters. It is very easy to use (and free). You can register for the channels of the work sought and the new offers are sent automatically to the mobile telephone.

5. Activating RSS alerts.

Once the candidate has decided upon the Twitter user who best suits his job search, he must consider the possibility of activating RSS and mobile alerts with a view to being among the first candidates to receive job offer messages, including text messages on the mobile phone.

In any case, there is a wide range of Twitter users who like to make job offers by field, company, region and more. To find recruiters to follow on Twitter, the candidate must make a search using keywords like "job offers", "seeking a job", etc.

Recommendations for managing a personal blog

These are the factors whereby one candidate's blog will stand out from the others and allow him to create a professional profile which suits his professional objectives:

1. Updating the blog: adding entries with news on given subject areas and answering readers' comments, writing value-adding content.

2. Reinventing yourself: new ideas, being original (not recycling other blogs), creating new activities from and for the blog.

3. Being the first in a specialist area and being consistent with regard to blogging.

4. Social skills for relating to others. For example, giving lectures or attending events.

5. Best practices must be followed: quoting sources, including links, etc.

2.0 platforms for professional profiles for candidates: *CV online*

DOYOUBUZZ
http://www.doyoubuzz.com

This allows the user (candidate) to draw up a CV by importing data from his LinkedIn account, for example, and also to synchronise this data with that appearing in his Facebook profile. This CV can be exported in Word or PDF and allows for the inclusion of images and videos, so that the design of the CV us more personalised and can even be translated into a variety of languages.

Other alternatives also exist on the market for creating our CV on the internet and providing a location for it:

VISUALCV
http://www.visualcv.com

This allows you to create a CV for the net, and as a starting point, it has an excellent visual appearance. It also allows you to store different file attachments within the CV, whether multimedia, such as video or audio, images or text documents in a wide range of formats. Another feature is that it offers the option of incorporating it into the social networks, offering the possibility of linking the CV as created to our accounts on LinkedIn, Facebook or Twitter. We can also create various types of CVs, adapted to the various profiles according to the position we would like to choose.

Once we have created the CV we intend to make accessible on the internet, we can set about distributing it via social networks: if we have linked the CV on Facebook, Twitter, LinkedIn or Xing, the options for getting ourselves known professionally begin to multiply.

Other websites exist on the internet designed to help create a CV: SmartCV or Europass.

When you innovate, you run the risk of making mistakes. It's best to quickly admit it and go on with another innovation.

Steve Jobs

All you learn from your successes is to think too much about yourself. All the progress you make always comes from failures, and when you've learned to recognise failure, admit it, learn from it, overcome it and try again.

Dee Hock (Founder of VISA International)

Knowing what is right and not doing it is the worst kind of cowardice.

Confucius

A man with a new idea is a very rare beast until the idea is a success.

Mark Twain

If the road is always clear, you've probably lost your way.

Charles Kettering

Social networks have become a new medium for recruiting talent in business. This being the case, users must be aware of what can be seen by anyone connecting to the internet, thus avoiding making the following common mistakes.

Therefore I tell you: know your enemy and know yourself;
in a hundred battles you will never be beaten. If you are
ignorant about your enemy but know yourself, your chances
of winning or losing are the same. If you are ignorant about
your enemy and about yourself, you can be sure
of losing every battle.

Sun Tzu

Most common errors in social networks to avoid by candidates:

1	The candidates (just like the companies) must think about the goal they wish to achieve before registering with a social network.
2	Use an email address that is neutral regarding access to social networks.
3	Ensure that the profile is 100% completed with updated information.
4	Take care with political and religious opinions.
5	Uploading compromising photographs or videos to an internet community.
6	Cultivating the contacts network and not accepting anyone who attempts to add you to theirs.
7	Configure privacy on social networks.
8	Remember to close the session.

1. The candidates (just like the companies) must think about the goal they wish to achieve before registering with a social network. A mistake made by some candidates is to register with all the social networks without working out whether they

are in a position to devote time to them or not. If a candidate is a CEO, manager or middle manager in various areas (human resources, marketing, logistics, etc.), and fits between technical profiles and specialists, he should be registered on LinkedIn, which is the worldwide number one network on which most management professionals are registered. If the candidate is looking for work in Germany, or is really a member of middle management, with a technical bias, he should favour registration on Xing. If the country where he is looking for a position is France, the most important professional network is Viadeo.

2. Use an email address that is neutral regarding access to social networks. Your registration and subsequent access will have an email address attached. It is not advisable to use the company email address (candidates nowadays with employment mobility cannot remain in the same company all their lives). This means that it is advisable to create a specific email account for the occasion (you can make use of Yahoo! or Gmail). Yahoo! account email addresses allow access to Delicious and Flickr, and Gmail accounts allow access to RSS readers, such as Feedly, among others.

3. Ensure that the profile is 100% completed with updated information. When a candidate makes out his profile on a professional social network such as LinkedIn, he should think about his CV and consider everything contained therein, since producing a profile that is not 100% complete produces an image of slackness, which is not seen as desirable by human resources officers. It is not just important to be on LinkedIn, you also have to have an attractive profile. We should bear in mind that it is a showcase for talent. Your profile is your business card.

4. Take care with political and religious opinions. Include content and take part in specialist groups which could give a candidate a competitive advantage over other potential

candidates, since it will help him gain visibility on the internet. This will cause some headhunters to focus on him and they may contact him about a future vacancy. Even so, it is then possible to adopt behavioural standards on the internet which could convert that visibility into a point of dispute with negative connotations which could lead to being sidelined at the first step in the selection process.

5. Uploading compromising photographs or videos to an internet community. Uploading and sharing photographs on a social network is very quick, easy and very dangerous. Never forget that a picture is worth a thousand words.

6. Cultivating the contacts network and not accepting anyone who attempts to add you to theirs. Accepting all invitations regardless is pointless. It is advisable to work out a strategy and some objectives, and above all to analyse profiles before accepting. You don't want mass contacts; you want qualified contacts. It is a fact that before launching a job search we never know who is going to help us, and it is for this reason that we must be clear about our goal, which could be adapted and varied depending on each moment in our working lives.

7. Configure privacy on social networks. You should remember that if you do not opt for privacy, the privacy levels of your profile and other information are by default very low. Spending the time you need to study and personalise to the maximum privacy on social networks is the key to an excellent management of your personal brand and digital reputation.

8. Remember to close the session. Many access actions recorded on social networks are from public computers. It is important to be careful (above all, when exiting from a social network, it should never be done by using the upper button with the cross); always look for the "Close session" or "Exit" link so that you are completely disconnected from the session.

Most common errors committed by candidates in job interviews:

1. The candidate is late.

2. The candidate is dishevelled.

3. The candidate is unprepared.

4. Candidate complains about previous employers.

5. Candidate left previous jobs for bad reasons.

6. Candidate can't provide a supervisor for a reference.

7. Candidate can't share about learning from a mistake.

8. Candidate is more interested in personal benefit.

9. Candidate is rude and/or dishonest.

10. Candidate has a bad attitude, very guarded and defensive.

11. Candidate is too enthusiastic.

Throughout this book we have concentrated to a greater extent on the professional social network LinkedIn rather then delving in detail into the features of Facebook, because it is a general network, but since it is the social network with the greatest number of users worldwide, human resources professionals should consider this network when it comes to branding, publishing job offers and interacting with potential candidates.

From this latter perspective, it is important to remember a few points of interest about privacy on Facebook for users/future candidates for the purpose of protecting their privacy and avoiding rejection in a selection process.

Who can see what you publish on Facebook?

If when registering with Facebook you accepted the recommendation to publish openly for "everybody" be default, that means that you have voluntarily authorised Facebook to share the information about the material you publish with any user or application on the website. Depending on your search options, it may be that you have also authorised Facebook to share that information with the search engines.

For example, in November 2007, a bank staff member in the U.S. was sacked for failing to come to work on the grounds of a family emergency when in reality on that very day he was celebrating Halloween. This was revealed by the photographs which appeared on Facebook.

This is also a clear example of the personal branding, or the digital identity of the candidate who, sadly for him, appeared on a number of websites wearing a Halloween costume, followed by the caption: "Employee fired for having been found on Facebook celebrating Halloween when he took a day off work claiming some family problem."

Is there such a thing as addiction to social networks?

If you're out of work, turning into a LinkedIn addict, or a LinkedInholic is almost certain. In fact, I think you ought to be one, because it's the best way to find a headhunter who might contact you.

Dan Schawbel

According to a study by Retrevo.com, most users of social networks, especially those possessing an iPhone, are addicted to their Twitter o Facebook accounts, which has now become their primary source of information and the reason for endless (welcome) interruptions.

With the popularisation of devices such as intelligent telephones, netbooks and the iPad, checking the news on social networks has moved on from being something you might do from time to time on a computer to what, at least for some, is a compulsive habit, since they are unable to stop themselves from following updates at any time and place.

From time to time the gadget-specialist website Retrevo.com surveys its clients to find out how the users use the technology in their daily lives. Even bearing in mind the fact that this is a particularly susceptible public, it is still somewhat surprising to realise the extent to which some people have become obsessed with Facebook, Twitter, YouTube and others.

For example, 16% of Twitter and Facebook users use these sources to find out the news every morning, to the detriment of traditional media such as the TV. The percentage rises to 23% among owners of an iPhone and of those, 28% check the news on their accounts even before getting out of bed.

The study "Is social media an addiction?" analyses the frequency with which users read the news on Twitter and Facebook and concludes:

– The majority (40% of those under 25 and 46% of the rest) are comfortable not checking the news for quite prolonged periods of time.

– Others (23 and 29%, respectively) check it once a day, while some lower percentages (20 and 15%) do it several times a day.

– The most hooked (18% and 11%) consult it every two hours.

The conclusion of the study is that we do not yet possess sufficient data to state that there exists a pathological addiction to social networks, but when a large proportion of the population checks their accounts at midnight, or it's the first thing they do in the morning when they get up, we can at least begin to talk about a chance in the way the communications media is being consumed.

New professions of the future arising from the 3.0 environment

The advantage always goes to the early riser.

Sun Tzu

Managers Magazine published a study in which technology consultant Gartner included their key predictions for social and collaborative software in business.

These predictions cover team collaboration and dynamic social networking applications, which offer a wide range of channels and content.

Mark R. Gilbert, Gartner research vice president, explains:

"In one year many things have changed in social software and the collaborative space. The growing popularity of platforms such as Twitter and Facebook in business has become a management drive to involve social software in the business environment. The success of social and collaborative software is characterised by an effort to find a place between information technologies and business."

According to Matt Cain, Gartner research vice president, "the rigid distinction between email and social networks will become blurred. Email will acquire many social attributes such as intermediary actions with contacts, while social networks will develop more complete messaging capabilities."

In this context, new professions are appearing in the 3.0 environment.

Here are a list of some new jobs related to the new Web 3.0:

- Big Data scientist

- Community manager.

- Security and avatar design specialist.

- Personal robot mechanic.

- Talent broker.

- Principal responsibility agent.

- Relationship marketing manager.

- Internet reputation head.

- Website analysis expert.

- Digital content manager.

- Digital information architect.

- Usability expert.

- SEO head.

- SEM head.

- Information architect.

4

Talent Search Strategy: Recruitment Plan 3.0. Legal Aspects

4.1. Recruitment Plan 3.0

"Would you tell me, please, which way I ought to go from here?"
"That depends a good deal on where you want to get to."
answered the Cheshire Cat.
"I don't much care where," said Alice.
"Then it doesn't much matter which way you go," said the Cat.

Lewis Carroll, *Alice in Wonderland*

According to the Talent Attraction and Selection Strategy, which every organisation should adopt, a variety of social networks and 3.0 tools can be incorporated.

The first step is to define the objectives, and then using them as a foundation, develop a strategy and make use of the social media tools that will help us to achieve those objectives.

Human resources policies should be aligned with the corporate strategy and should then adopt the 2.0 tools which best suit our objectives.

What tools, such as social networks, can we use in a human resources strategy? LinkedIn, Xing, Facebook, Twitter?

– In the first place, we must concentrate on those social networks where our potential employees are to be found. The main opportunity offered by these social networks is to organise our candidates into a classification which in the past was not possible.

– In the second place, we must be aligned with the 2.0 marketing strategy (attracting customers), since this can be extrapolated and can have a practical application in the human resources 2.0 strategy (attracting talent).

Human resources professionals must talk to their marketing and communications colleagues, as they were the pioneers in making maximum use of social networks to attract customers, because as well as exploiting synergies, they would be aligned with the corporate strategy.

And anyway, in the short term it is the human resources professionals who will have to organise marketing campaigns to attract talent, something we referred to at the beginning of the book as employer branding.

We can see that the new trend in the talent attraction strategy is to have an active and quality presence on social networks. Companies must sow the seed (in other words, they must be present on social networks and interact with potential candidates, whether they are selected or not) in order to harvest the fruits in the future, that is, they must have an excellent employer brand image as a provider of employment and a pool of potential candidates.

"The good farmer knows how to wait for the sowing season, and does not forget."

Also of interest is the fact that companies, via their blogs and presence on social networks, are able to advise potential candidates about their employment concerns. It is also advisable to publicise events that favour the relationship between the company and potential candidates on the internet. The new age of transparency has arrived.

In his book *Second to One: How Our Smartest Companies Put People First,* Charles Garfield includes the following statement:

> *I believe that there really has to exist in all good companies (...)*
> *a mutual relationship with the employees. It is essential to work*
> *with their interests at heart... and in the long run,*
> *this will be to the advantage of the company.*
>
> Sam Walton (founder of Walmart)

In the new jobs market, companies make use of employer branding strategies to attract talent to their organisations, and "the offer of value to the employee" together with the new forms of behaviour of the candidates in the employment market (the number of professionals who use social networks to seek jobs is constantly growing) open the way to 3.0 recruitment.

According to Dan Schawbel, expert in personal branding, author of *Me 2.0: Build a Powerful Brand to Achieve Career Success,* the economic scenario forces everyone to be an expert in their field.

It is becoming increasingly necessary to be creative in order to stand out from the crowd. If companies do not see their teams as ambassadors of their own brand, they run the risk of seeing their talent move away to other companies.

When recruiting each professional, the HR officer must be clear that there exists a vision and a shared mission, and brand qualities. If talent which can become incorporated into the culture of the company is not recruited, it may soon abandon the organisation and ruin the corporate environment. The idea is that once the right employees have been recruited, they must be trained in everything that is related to the values of the company, and they must be allowed to use social networks to build their brand and support the company mission.

In the future, human resources professionals will have to learn to optimise their social networks as a fundamental channel for recruitment, possibly the only one. They will have to learn an infinity of new things and basically move around on the internet with greater agility than before, and they will even have to respond more rapidly to applicants (making use of the new technological advances which allow them to automate responses - autoreply, etc.), since if they fail to do so they will create the image of an obsolete company, hence one which is unattractive to new talent.

Obviously, this is a great opportunity for companies that can play this new game before the others.

With this in mind, some Spanish companies have provided themselves with two community managers (CMs): one reporting to the marketing and communications area, the other to human resources. Sometimes there is just one CM operating with respect to both areas (marketing and human resources).

The marketing and communications areas must be aligned with the human resources section as a key point for building a sound employer branding strategy that will be credible along with the external brand, which is transmitted to the customers. The entire approach will help to a great extent to create commitment and confidence in the values of the organisations. The secret is to construct these values in a coherent form and communicate them to all levels of the organisation.

"You can never prevent a great catastrophe, but you can build an organisation which is ready for battle, with high morale, which

knows how to behave, which has confidence in itself, where the people trust each other. In military training, the first rule is to imbue your soldiers with trust in their officers, because if they don't trust them, they will not fight."

Peter Druker (in *Managing the Non-Profit Organisation: Principles and Practices*)

Web 2.0, unlike internet 1.0, has an architecture which provides a democratic participation structure, encouraging participation, trust and the sharing of ideas, while stimulating conversations and networking.

In this sense, analysts like Andrew McAfee, a researcher from the Massachusetts Institute of Technology (MIT), highlights the fact that new technologies perform a function which goes beyond socialisation, because it allows for the harvesting of the knowledge dispersed throughout the organisation and the generation of ideas.

The recruitment 3.0 strategy is based on four principles: collaboration, technology, innovation, and transparency.

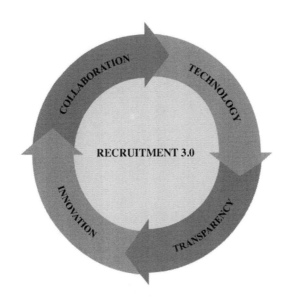

According to the LinkedIn survey "Global Recruiting Trends":

Broader technology advancements have also begun to disrupt the talent industry, setting the stage for a dynamic and exciting future for recruiting.

Advancement	Implication for Recruiting
Social Media	The accessibility and connectedness of professionals online has made talent more accessible than ever.
Digital Marketing	With digital marketing tools, organizations can now segment and target talent with relevant jobs and messages on a massive scale.
Mobile	With the rise of mobile device usage, candidates now research and apply for work in a mobile-optimized format.
Machine Learning	Adaptive algorithms match jobs with professionals based on profile demographics and real-time behavioral feedback.
Big Data Analytics	As data storage and processing become cheaper, talent acquisition leaders can become strategic advisors to the business by arming themselves with data.

Human resources professionals are aware of the potential of social communication media technologies in the workplace and in their private and professional lives.

Nowadays, new technologies allow companies to interact with people in a way that is open, fast and transparent, with a view to promoting their own brand, using the new Web 2.0 instruments.

"Sound reputations arise when companies are transparent in the way in which they do their business."

Charles Fombrum (author of *Reputation)*

And Sally Bibb and Jeremy Kourdi, in their book *Trust Matters: for Organisational and Personal Success,* include the following quotation:

"Try to be transparent, clear and truthful. Even when it's difficult, and above all when it's difficult."

Jean-Cyril Spineta (president and managing director of Air France)

The company website and the intranet should nowadays create an environment via which communication between the company and the various individuals with which it does business is managed, in which the relationships between the employees and the company and the outside customers are created, and in which the customer, including potential customers, can find a place to share knowledge and experience and even refer friends and family members to take part in the talent selection process.

This means that it is necessary to create networks by means of instruments (blogs, wikis, etc.) which put the company customers and employees in contact with each other, encouraging them to interact in a conversation which produces and distributes content.

"Spectacular successes are always the outcome of spectacular preparations."

How is a 3.0 Recruitment Plan organised?

The first stage of the 3.0 Recruitment Plan consists of identifying and locating the candidates in order to reveal which internet communities they are interested

Identifying the profiles of the candidates

Before we plunge into the depths of social media, we should identify which candidates are those we would like to recruit via the internet and ask three essential question: Who are they? Where are they? What language do they speak?

Who are they?	Where are they?	What language do they speak?
It engineer	LinkedIn	Spanish
Commercial	Xing	English
Administration	Viadeo	Chinese
Accounting	Twitter	Arabic
Financial manager	Blogs	French
Etc.	Etc.	Etc.

Preparing the tools

Throughout this book certain 2.0 tools have been mentioned repeatedly as being of practical use in attracting and selecting talent:

- General social networks: Facebook, Google+

- Professional social networks: LinkedIn, Xing, Viadeo.

- LinkedIn, with the activation of a profile of the company, together with personal profiles for each department head or manager. One or more groups covering company activities should also be activated.

- Microblogging networks (Twitter), with the activation of a company account on Twitter to publish job offers and news of interest. Each account can be private, allowing access only to human resources team members or the community manager.

- Bookmarks and aggregators; Delicious will allow you to store and classify the websites that the user may need in the development of the 2.0 recruitment plan.

- Corporate Blog, on which interaction is as much between company members as with employees or potential candidates, so that direct, lively and constant contact is maintained.

- RSS (Real Simple Syndication), with the activation of an RSS section on the company blog so that potential candidates can see the latest updates of the job offers, among other things.

- RSS feeds reader: Feedly is an example of a feeds reader which helps the user to follow all the updates of the websites with which he is registered: newspapers and specialist publications, blogs, etc.

- Video: having a corporate YouTube channel available on which you can publish videos like "Work With Us" to attract talent to the company.

- Wiki allows you to organise information by projects or manage the potential candidates' frequent question (FAQs) section, with content and organisation provided by the relevant team, enriching the resulting discourse as much with the company's in-house know-how as talent.

Defining potential candidates' keywords

Once we have worked out which candidates we want to look for on the internet, we should use keywords to find them. We will have to perform an empathy exercise (such as company name, profession, sector) and run a search on these keywords.

It is important to realise that the 3.0 recruitment strategy is a long-term procedure with success lasting over time and producing a better ROI.

There are some cases in which the use of very limited resources has produced a very high ROI.

Return on investment (ROI) in social media

What cannot be measured cannot be improved.

Joseph M. Juran

The ROI can be calculated with respect to social media, using this formula:

$$ROI = \frac{\text{Returned value} - \text{Initial value invested}}{\text{Initial value invested}}$$

Some of the parameters related to ROI are:

1. Initial investment. To work out the resources we are investing in our 2.0 recruitment strategy, we must factor in human and technological resources and the time required.

2. Objectives. Defining the objectives is crucial. Some objectives might be to make contact with a given number of future candidates, to secure new contacts, to set up links with our website, to increase our positioning and to improve our reputation on the internet.

3. Measurement tools. Although we cannot compare the data which these tools provide with a cash value, they can be of great value to use to relate to ROI: internet traffic, visits, new users, number of comments, fans on Facebook, followers on Twitter, etc.

According to a recent study by McKinsey & Company on the effectiveness of companies 2.0 or fully networked enterprises and the ROI generated by Social Web or Web 2.0, 69% of respondents said they received benefits by applying 2.0

strategies in their organizations: more innovative products and services, more effectivity in their marketing campaigns, reduced costs and increased profits. The conclusions from the results are:

- Benefits related to internal costs: 77% considers that the access to knowledge/training speed was increased, making use of social networking in the organization; 60% said that communication costs were reduced; 44% has reduced travel costs; 41% has increased satisfaction of employees.

- Benefits related to clients: 63% considers that their marketing campaigns have been most effective and 50% that it has increased customer satisfaction.

Moreover, the results of a recent report by Marketing Sherpa show that in organizations that use social media, the ROI average is 95%, but even some exceed this percentage, 12% reached 200% ROI and 2% reached 1,000%.

The results of these and other surveys about the benefits and the ROI of applying 2.0 strategies are positive both internally with employees and externally with customers, suppliers and partners.

Why use social networks in attracting and recruiting talent?

We can simplify and highlight three reasons for using social web recruitment:

– Search for candidates.

– Build relationships with potential candidates or communities of interest.

– Creation of a brand as an employer or employer branding.

What are the metrics to measure ROI in social media?

- **Influence:** The influence on social media as a recruiter is great, its scope to reach a larger audience will be greater. To measure the influence there are 2.0 tools like Klout or Twitalyzer.

- **Traffic:** The influence will have an impact on traffic, no doubt. When an organization shares on the networks links to job offers, the clicks on those links can be measured through tools like Google Analytics, to know where the traffic is going. Another tool, Wakoopa, measures time and the real use of Facebook, Twitter, etc.

- **Conversations:** This metric is related to the conversations and comments in social media about an organization. To monitor this metric you can use, Klout, Glassdoor and configure Google Alerts with the keywords of the company (name, sector, etc.). Social networks are a great help to companies to reduce the costs of recruitment talent, improve their visibility as employer branding, encouraging their growth and adaptation to the new generations of talent.

Companies need applications whereby they can measure each sale that is generated via Twitter, Facebook or the corporate blog. In order to do this they use the Key Performance Indicators (KPI), which are the indicators used to measure the achievement of their objectives, such as:

- Reputation.

- Good name.

- Website traffic.

- Time the user is connected.

We can measure the engagement with social platforms.

- Account ownership.

- Visitation.

- Active usage.

A software package has been developed in the U.S. which is used to measure the ROI on social networks, among other features: Hubspot http://www.hubspot.com

HR Metrics: KPI´s for Recruitment

- **Time to fill.** Number of days from which the job requisition was approved to the hire start date.

- **Hire ratio.** Number of employees hired per month ÷ total number of employees hired per year.

- **Offer letter acceptance rate.** Number of offer letters accepted ÷ all offer letters extended.

To measure the ROI in social media we can follow the next three steps:

1. Goals: Consider what you value the most and how much each source costs; ratio application to first-interview, cost-per-hire, time-per-hire, etc.

2. Benchmark: If you're hiring for different types of roles in different geographical locations or areas of specialization (IT, Sales, Marketing positions, etc.)

3. Credit the source: Be sure you can track candidates coming from that source. Only when the social channel you want to evaluate can be fully tracked automatically (for example:

integrated with your Applicant Tracking System -ATS) then you can see real conclusions of effectiveness.

Integration with the ATS: Most Applicant Tracking Systems (ATS) automatically post open positions to job search engines. Most of the companies that are using social media to attract new talent use a direct feed from the ATS to the job search engines; then they're assured that their most recent openings are reaching candidates. On the other hand, if a company is not leveraging this direct connection to an ATS, and is using only job boards to advertise openings, then it runs the risk that candidates are seeking outdated positions in the job board's database.

Recommendations on the creation and development of HR strategy 3.0:

1	Align human resource strategies with marketing.
2	Transparency and collaboration.
3	Be creative and different from others.
4	Employer branding, employee value proposition.
5	Personal branding: personal branding candidate on the network.
6	Innovation.
7	Training for HR teams.
8	Be active and have quality presence in Web 2.0.
9	Consider four principles.
10	Be the first.

1. **Align human resource strategies with marketing.** HR professionals should talk to their colleagues in marketing and the communication area, which have been the pioneers in making the most of social networks to attract customers. In addition to leveraging synergies, they will align with corporate strategy.

2. **Transparency and collaboration:** It is advisable that companies, through their presence in social networks, promote the relationship between company and potential candidates.

3. **Be creative and different from others:** For example, some companies have used Business Games to attract talent.

4. **Employer branding, employee value proposition:** The brand creation strategy must be developed from the HR area to attract talent, "the employee value proposition".

   It is also recommended that companies see their employees as ambassadors of their own organization.

5. **Personal branding: personal branding candidate on the network:** At the time of selecting each professional we must be sure that there is a common vision and mission. Social networks allow viewing personal branding in the network of a candidate.

6. **Innovation:** Companies, through HR professionals, will have to innovate by marketing campaigns to attract talent.

7. **Training for HR teams:** In the coming years, HR professionals must learn to optimize social networks as a key channel for recruitment and to move through Web 2.0 with more agility than before. They even must respond more quickly to the candidates that are applying.

8. **Be active and have quality presence in Web 2.0:** We can see that the new trend in strategy for attracting and recruiting talent 2.0 will be having an active and quality presence on social networks. Control of digital reputation.

9. **Consider four principles:** The recruitment strategy 2.0 is based on four principles or basic seeds: collaboration, technology, innovation and transparency.

10. **Be the first:** Obviously, it is a great opportunity for companies that play this new game 2.0 first.

Next, some recommendations for a 3.0 effective recruitment plan are highlighted:

1	Know the business.
2	Define the goals.
3	Define the company culture.
4	Define the most appropriate social networks.
5	Know the statistics of social networking use.
6	Diagnosis of the company and industry benchmarking.
7	Time management.
8	Content management.
9	Action plan and measuring results.

1. **Know the business:** Understanding the purpose of business is the key to choosing the most appropriate social networks and establishing an effective Web 2.0 strategy. In some cases, businesses make the mistake of being in too many social networks without considering the nature of the business they are in.

2. **Define the goals:** Setting goals is the key (for example, search for candidates, employer branding, etc.) and the time must be limited to short term (in a quarter), medium term (in one year) and long term (more than one year).

3. **Define the company culture:** First you should check if the mission, vision and values that a company has published (usually in their web or intranet) are considered as a "real culture of the company" for current employees and otherwise must work gradually to align the mission, vision and values the company would like to have and perform related action plan.

4. **Define the most appropriate social networks:** Establish social networks to use depending on the goals. You do not always have to be in all social networks at once, but you can start with those in which your candidates really are and gradually expand according to plan. According to the Social Recruiting Survey 2011. Job Seeker Nation 2010, 64% of companies use two or more social networks to recruit talent in the network: first, LinkedIn, secondly, Facebook and, thirdly, Twitter. It is also important to know international social networks by country.

5. **Know the statistics on social networking use:** By profile, country, etc. Next, we highlight some demographic statistics of the three major social networks: LinkedIn (42% female and 58 % men), Facebook (51% female and 49% male), Twitter (43% women and 57% men).

6. **Diagnosis of the company and industry benchmarking:** To make an analysis of the presence in the Web 2.0, we must resolve the following questions: What information systems and / or social networks in their case, are being used? Is there a monitoring / tracking system of applicants? The social reputation of the company must be studied and

if a company is not present in the networks that does not mean it does not have a digital reputation.

7. **Time management:** To make a 2.0 recruitment plan requires time, effort and persistence. Due to the increase of information processed and the many tasks that we develop daily, sometimes we do not devote enough time to organizing these tasks and becoming more efficient. According to Pareto's Principle, also known as the 80/20 rule, 80% of the effects come from 20% of the causes.

   Use the Pareto Principle to analyse a situation and facilitate making strategic decisions working with real data (Eg use of the networks that are more suitable for our personal / corporate) objectives. According to the survey "Social networks for more efficient selection 2.0", carried out in the U.S. by Jobvite, the network LinkedIn is the network that offers best results. Moreover, and also related to time management, one of the biggest mistakes companies make in social selection is having a limited time plan. Time management and consistency are the key, which is why it is important to answer the following questions: how much time do we actually have or propose to have for selection through social networks? 40, 30, 20, 15 or 5 hours a week? Who or what department will be responsible for communication in social networks?

8. **Content management:** This is one of the areas on which human resources often spend less. In the company's marketing and communication areas that are in the Web 2.0, they follow the 75-25 rule, which means that 25% of the content must be information about the company and the remaining 75% on news and information related to the company. However, this rule does not apply 100% to recruitment 2.0 because potential candidates want to know more information about the company where they are interested in working. Therefore, the following percentage distribution can be made:

- 25% of information about the culture of the company and employer brand.

- 50% of concrete information on vacancies and how to access the recruitment process.

- 25% of information about news and information regarding the company and /or sector.

9. **Action plan and measuring results:** The plan must specify dates and estimated times of work (defined daily, weekly, monthly, etc.) and the moment when new targets must be established. It is essential to know the results to measure the cost-benefit ratio of the investment, so you should always include a detailed explanation of how to measure and present the results, and how often this will be done. They can be measured by objectives, cost savings for the company, improving the company image (employer branding), per work hour, month, week, etc. The recommendation is, like in previous points, to be accurate and give more detailed information of the breakdown of working hours, the time value or the value of each goal, and to know why we are paying and /or the dedicated human resources.

Companies can increase their pool of knowledge and skills by adding new talent. The decision of hiring talent relies on four dimensions:

1. Competencies

2. Motivation

3. Adaptability

4. References

Some recommendations for HR 2.0 professionals are:

1	Develop a 2.0 communication strategy.
2	Develop a branding strategy.
3	Check your reputation.
4	Streamline in-house collaboration.
5	Keep up to date with human resources
6	Diagnosis of the company and industry benchmarking.
7	Time management.

1. Develop a 2.0 communication strategy: To do so, it is important to draw up a social networks usage code whereby you can clearly point out to employees what is acceptable and what is not with regard to the use of social networks in the workplace.

2. Develop a branding strategy. Use social communications networks for employer branding. High quality content should appear on the corporate website in various formats (audio, video, blogs, articles) and should link up with social networks which have a presence in the company. Create high quality content on Web 2.0.

3. Check your reputation. Human resources professionals are aware of the power of social media in the hiring process and that it works in both directions. What do the candidates, customers and employees say about a company? Google alerts are very useful for human resource professionals. Registering with a reputation management service is also becoming essential for any company keen to know what is being said about it.

4. Streamline in-house collaboration. Using tools such as in-house blogs helps employees improve in-house communications and teamwork. Collaborative participation upgrades productivity and commitment indices.

5. Keep up to date with human resources news by subscribing to some blogs, such as Tom Peters (http://www.tompeters.com) or Dan Schawbel's, specialising in personal branding (http://www.personalbrandingblog.com).

6. Don't be afraid to think differently. Would we, for example, recommend the worldwide use of Warcraft as a tool for developing leadership? It is more than likely that the answer for the great majority of human resources professionals would be no. And yet an article in the *Harvard Business Review* expressed its support for this initiative.

7. Include in the corporate website "Work With Us" section all the social networks and 2.0 tools where the company has a presence: This is not only an excellent way to render the information viral, ensuring that it reaches a large number of potential candidates, but it also helps keep the presence of the company on social networks compiled and ordered, on a single website on the official corporate employment page. It should not be forgotten that the first website visited by a potential candidate is the official corporate website, so this should be the centre of the recruitment strategy and should indicate the links to social networks.

Web 3.0. and social networks have streamlined (time and cost saving) international recruitment.

International talent search 3.0. Example:

How can you manage an international process involving a country manager in Dubai and a customer in Barcelona, sold by the UK office and executed by a consultant in India? How is the search strategy to be designed for a country manager in the oil and gas sector in Dubai?

As recently as seven years ago a candidate selection process in Dubai would probably have been impossible without an office in the country. Thanks to technology, and mainly the internet, not only is it now possible, but production time and costs are also lower.

The new 3.0. recruitment tools have made it possible to find candidates in any corner of the globe and have cut selection process times into the bargain.

The steps to follow:

- First, we identify the target public of the competing companies at the world level and the local level of our client to locate the most suitable candidate for the position to be filled. We also investigate companies in sectors parallel to the oil and gas sector, where we might be able to find qualified professionals. We identify the companies of the final candidates in oil and gas procedures who have been successful in developing their projects and offer them to the client as an example of best practice.

- Second, once the horizon of companies where these professionals can be located is defined, the new 2.0 recruitment techniques for identifying professionals come into play.

- The following types of recruitment means are designed and activated. There are several options:

- Looking for the most effective social media tools: LinkedIn groups of professionals at the local and international level, Facebook groups, mention in Twitter specific and influential users.

- Specific employee career sites

- At the local level, Chambers of Commerce, associations, business schools and universities.

- At HR analytics: using Big Data

A presence on social networks opens many doors for you when you come to a country or region which is initially unknown to you, as it brings you closer to its people, its customs, culture and traditions.

In the Middle East region it is possible that the positive impact and return on investment may be still greater, from the westerner's point of view, since you find it easier to understand the standards and customs of the country or region you are approaching.

A very important factor to bear in mind is that not all the social networks are alike, nor do they make use of identical systems of relations. This means that it is advisable first to analyse the network where you are registered in order to find out what codes of conduct have been established to users to relate to each other, since the forms of behaviour adopted by LinkedIn, Facebook or Twitter users are not the same.

According to the model of leadership: The "Extraordinary and Inspirational Leader", described by Zenger/Folkman, has remained in place, and has empirically demonstrated that the most powerful leadership skill is that of "inspiring and motivating others to greater effort"; and the use of social networks as channels for identifying and securing these professionals is of ever greater importance, since this makes for interaction, cooperation and finally two-way effectiveness.

The headhunting team of Global Human Capital Group http://www.globalhumancapitalgroup.com, adds:

"A very recent successful case we recently experienced at Global Human Capital Group in the use of 3.0. recruitment was the search for an industrial engineer in aluminium extrusion for the Saudi Arabia delegation of a Spanish multinational in the industrial sector.

In this case, success was based on the possibility of accessing a large number of contacts and the speed with which the most suitable candidate was found.

If we had faced this situation 10 years ago, it would have taken us over two months to cover it and we would have identified very few candidates.

On this occasion, with the help of Employee career sites, LinkedIn and its groups, and Twitter, the information turned viral so that in a week we had identified 500 contacts and within less than a month we had finished the selection and the candidate was in place.

A personnel selection model that does not involve social networks and the Web 3.0. environment as essential elements is nowadays unthinkable.

Advantages of the use of social networks in the business of attracting and recruiting talent:

1. Unprecedented direct access to the best talent in the world.

2. The data they offer is usually very up to date, but the level of detail of the professional profile varies a great deal, and depends on what the professional decides to reveal.

3. Finding and contacting highly qualified contacts in a passive manner.

4. Making it possible for users to publish their CV and professional profile, to create a network of contacts and to access job offers before they are published by other media.

5. They are internet tools, so they are always available and offer good search engines (by sector, company keywords).

6. They create your employer branding in accordance with stated objectives, since it is possible to access specialist or vertical social networks, specialist groups on LinkedIn for publishing job offers, etc.

7. They create a unique company profile.

8. They save effort, time and money and a potentially worldwide audience is reached.

9. They particularly focus on middle management, managers, executives of decision-making positions, with a wide geographical and sector variety.

10. The system is free of charge (although the so-called premium services offering added services do exist).

If access to professional social networks is free of charge, and they are effective in tracking down the profiles of experts, does this mean that specialist consultants in locating executives and headhunters will disappear?

They will not disappear, but the volume of business handled by headhunters in recent years (2009-2016) is down by between 30 and 50%. Headhunting outfits are going to have to reinvent themselves to adapt to the new 3.0. environment.

Possible objections to 3.0 recruiting: How can business be persuaded of this change of mentality?

> *Resistance to new ideas is proportional to the square of their importance.*
> Bertrand Russell

> *Men build too many walls and few bridges.*
> Isaac Newton

If you don't like change, you'll really hate being irrelevant.

Eric Shinseki

The old models of attracting and recruiting talent are now becoming obsolete, because talent is not to be found in the same way as it was years ago.

However, the new 2.0 recruitment model has not yet become fully developed in every organisation, since it demands new skills and specific training for the professionals in the selection field.

Ignorance of the matter in most cases where it is found means that cases of resistance are numerous and usually tragically misguided because of that very ignorance.

These are the four most common areas of resistance:

1. The belief that social networks are only used to recruit young people. This is not the case, and indeed if we look for candidates on LinkedIn, for example, we will find that the vast majority of the profiles are graduates, technical professionals, middle management and managers. There is a wide age spread, and in addition to the younger candidate we shall also find professionals with lengthy professional experience.

2. The belief that methodologies, which were successful at some given moment in the past, will work in the future. This is a false premise, because it assumes that you can play a new game but use the old rules. Outdated methods in a 2.0 environment are not compatible with organisational success.

3. The belief that finding out how to use the 2.0 tools is complicated. The origin of this type of resistance is the rejection of the new, which required that new skills be taken on. Being a good social network user means knowing

how to generate and manage virtual communities, how to communicate in a different way by handling direct contacts, and by always adopting the position of the employer brand ambassador.

4. The belief that the company reputation will be affected if it appears on social networks. This belief is incorrect since companies are also exposed to the comments of other users. People will comment on the company whether it is a member of social networks or not, which means that it is important to build a sound, credible and orientated brand creation strategy on the basis of the company values and culture, in order to attract the talent to be found on the internet in a direct way.

The main barriers to the establishment of this kind of information exchange are associated with the behaviour guidelines and standards laid down within a company.

The greater the extent of hierarchy in a business, the harder it will be to adapt. Organisations are becoming more "net-archical" as they adapt themselves to the new generations.

It is almost never too late to do what you ought to have done.

George Eliot

The ancient battleships of the industrial era will founder, battered by the waves, while the companies which build lighter structures, interconnected on the internet, and succeed in connecting up to external ideas and energies, will achieve the buoyancy needed to survive.

The companies which anticipate these changes and lead them will obtain important advantages in their sectors.

Don Tapscott and Anthony D. Williams (Wikinomics)

In his article "How to Sell Marketing on the Social Networks to Your Boss", published in RWWES, internet marketing guru

Jeff Bullas offers serious advice for the use of social media for companies. Since his view is that of the U.S. market, some of his recommendations will be inappropriate for our case, so we have selected the following suggestions as to how to convince our bosses that they should incorporate social networks into their business.

To these we have added the recommendations made by Andrew McAfee.

1. Show them what they are doing wrong: For example, by making a search on Google and finding that the company does not appear on the first page.

2. Show them data on companies: Practical cases, surveys and best practices, which have been successful in the use of social media.

3. Show them data on the scope and reach of social media.

4. Take the first step: This can be as simple as suggesting that they open a blog and publish the content there that already exists on physical supports. This will also help them to be better positioned on Google.

5. Suggest some good reasons why a CEO might benefit from the use of social media:

    *   Boosting interaction with, and proximity to, customers (potential candidates);

    *   Opening dialogue with potential customers, thus giving the brand greater credibility;

- Reading directly what consumers/potential employees think about our brand;

- Accelerating the actions of our brand in traditional media;

- Adapting the language of our brand to connect with new customers/potential employees;

- Always keeping abreast of the latest news in the industry and the world in general;

- Sharing their experience as a CE and professional in the sector (which is very highly valued in this medium);

- Setting right any incorrect statements about the brand;

- Boosting business and launching low-budget campaigns;

- Establishing a brand with an opinion;

- Boosting the impact of direct marketing (website SEO);

- Direct connections with the main media and analysts;

- Approaching all generations, races, creeds and countries to contact a public which no other channel could contemplate reaching.

There's no point in hiring intelligent people and them telling them what to do. We hire intelligent people so that they can tell us what to do.

Steve Jobs

Most common errors in social networks for employers to avoid

1	Access being denied to social networks at the workstation.
2	Believing that all profiles are to be found on the social networks.
3	Use of a social network unsuited to the position to be filled.
4	Defining corporate goals before applying 2.0 tools.
5	Return on investment (ROI).
6	Transparency in communication.

1. Access being denied to social networks at the workstation, since in some companies corporate policy is to limit access. In some cases, employees use the networks to build up contacts, which can give rise to potential new customers for the business, potential new candidates, and so on. It would be better for companies if they were to incorporate standards for social networks into their corporate policy and their procedures manual (bearing in mind that only 10% of them possess a procedures manual), thus making it clear what is acceptable and what is not in their organisation. We can remember the beginnings of the internet, a time when nobody knew how useful it was going to be. The initial reaction of the majority of companies was to limit and control access to it, since it was seen as a way of wasting time and lowering productivity. Nowadays a company without internet access is unthinkable. The same will happen with social networks.

2. Believing that all profiles are to be found on social networks. *Not* all profiles are found on social networks. There exist profiles of candidates who are not familiar with the technology and are not to be found on Web 2.0. It is also certain that in the next few years anyone not on a social network will be seen

as someone not adapted to the new environment. The profiles of top management in other countries, such as the U.S., are present on networks such as LinkedIn.

3. Use of a social network unsuited to the position to be filled. Select the social network that best suits your interests. Before registering, we must think carefully about our objectives and choose those networks that will be most effective as regards to our ends. Talent spotting professionals will know that on LinkedIn they will find management, middle management and technical profiles. On Xing they will find technical and middle management profiles. On Facebook they will find the majority of the candidates who belong to Generation Y, and on Tuenti most youngsters belonging to Generation Z.

4. Defining corporate goals before applying 2.0 tools. Some companies do not set their goals in the human resources and marketing areas, and in some cases these objectives are not aligned. In the early days of Web 2.0 it was possible to observe some companies that had different corporate groups on the same social network with the same goals, which led to overlapping and an uncoordinated image of the network in the minds of management. This happened because most of the directors of these companies are not registered with social networks. Now that new professions have appeared, such as community manager, companies can deploy their 2.0 recruitment strategy with greater smoothness and in alignment with the marketing section to create synergies. First of all, businesses must create spaces that they will tackle, since the effect of not paying attention to potential candidates may be the opposite of what is needed.

5. Return on investment (ROI): The results of the implementation of a 2.0 recruitment strategy are in most cases measurable in the long term. Companies must not invest in social networks

expecting immediate results, since social networks are based on building relationships with potential candidates. What is, however, certain, is that from time to time on some social networks, such as LinkedIn, a direct candidate search can be undertaken without an initial investment.

6. Transparency in communication: Companies will achieve better results on social networks if they act with transparency, since they will create trust and establish their digital identity. Companies should not be afraid of sharing information with their potential candidates, like photographs of the office, tweets in real time during corporate events, slideshare presentations and videos on YouTube explaining the corporate values and benefits of working for the company, etc.

Providers of recruitment services

Employee Referrals
https://www.employeereferrals.com

Founded in early 2011 EmployeeReferrals.com has quickly grown to become the industry leader in employee referral services. Jobs have been shared with over 1 million people and jobs have been matched with over 50 million connections.

Global Human Capital Group
https://www.globalhumancapitalgroup.com

It is a job portal where companies can post their job offers and each can be shared on major social networks: LinkedIn, Twitter, Facebook, etc. It also has a RSS channel where the candidates can subscribe and receive job alerts on their mobile devices.

For more information: info@globalhumancapitalgroup.com

Jibe
https://www.jibe.com

This is a 2.0 employment website which checks the data on Facebook and LinkedIn to find job offers, and uses filters for sectors and geographical areas. Job-seekers can register/ identify themselves via either of the two social networks (LinkedIn or Facebook), and in this way they can update the profile on Jibe by automatically importing the data from LinkedIn. Some client companies are: AT&T, MTV, HP, Amazon, Bank of America, Conde Nast, Intel and Merck, among others.

Jobvite
http://www. jobvite.com

Jobvite is the first 2.0 selection platform (SaaS) that allows candidates to interact in the selection process. It is connected to LinkedIn, Twitter and Facebook. Human resources professionals include the links in the job offers they publish. Their clients include Starbucks, Logitech, Zappos and Mozilla. According to Anne Murguia, VP Marketing Jobvite:

"The tool is free of charge and user-friendly for any company which uses social networks. Jobvite features a real-time social network search engine and is used to produce statistics from them."

Resumark
http://www.resumark.com

This is a CV search engine using Google technology.

Resumark has a patented concept that allows candidates who are looking for jobs to earn money while searching: simply by sending their CV on line. Their privacy is protected at the same time. The 2.0 employment network helps with finding a better job and in less time.

The procedure, which is very simple, is as follows:

1. Send in your CV or create it on line: candidates are paid every time an employer downloads their CV.

2. Employers pay a dollar every time they download a CV. With a view to protecting the privacy of the candidates, the employers who obtain access to the contact's information are identified.

3. Users can invite friends to upload their CVs onto Resumark and the employers pay 50 cents every time they download a friend's CV.

Simply Hired: http://www.simplyhired.com

Simply Hired is one of the largest employment search engines. Its plan is to create the best search tool for finding work in the most simple and efficient way possible. It uses the RSS in a way that allows candidates to receive the vacancies which best match their profiles if they subscribe to the RSS.

Since it was set up in the U.S. in 2005, it has been working to harvest job offers from the best work forums, content sites, newspapers, company training organisations and websites to make up a powerful jobsearch website. Its unique tool, "Who Do I Know™", allows users to discover their friends and personal contacts in each company along with their jobsearch results. It also has a link with LinkedIn and Facebook applications.

Another website similar to Simply Hired is Indeed: http://www.indeed.

According to the Silkroad report *"Top Sources of Hire 2016: The Definitive Report on Talent Acquisition Strategies"*, Indeed remains the leader. Indeed is the most productive external source of interviews and hires. Indeed delivered more than six times as many interviews as CareerBuilder, the next largest external source. Moreover, it yielded nearly two and half times as many hires as all the other top branded external sources combined, i.e. CareerBuilder, Craigslist, LinkedIn, and Monster. A year-over-year analysis showed that Indeed continued to dominate the category of external sources, and it jumped 10% as a source of external interviews since last year. This wasn't entirely a surprise, since Indeed attracts a large pool of talent – claiming 180 million visitors a month from over 50 countries. Moreover, it has a strong mobile application, which enables job seekers to submit resumes, complete job applications, and answer qualifying questions.

4.2. Legal aspects: Policies for the use of social networks in companies

According to a survey carried out by SHSM with Society for Human Resources Management:

What kinds of professionals are primarily responsible for creating the social media policy for an organization?

43% Human Resources
17% Information Technology
11% Corporate or senior management
9% Marketing
8% Legal
8% Public Relations
4% Other

What kinds of professionals are primarily responsible for leading the social media policy for an organization?

35% Marketing
17% Information Technology
14% Human Resources

14% Corporate or senior management
13% Public Relations
4% Other
3% Sales

Below, thanks to the generosity of the International Financial Institution BBVA Group for their contribution to this book, we show the Social Media Policy which BBVA applies to its employees, and which might serve as an example to companies interested in establishing similar policies in their organisations:

"Guide to the use of the profiles/pages/corporate groups on social networks"

Encompassing all the standards is the BBVA Code of Conduct and the Communication Framework developed by Communications and Branding, which regulates the framework within which all messages being sent out by BBVA should pass. The visual materials used to identify ourselves as a brand should be approved by the Identity department.

General standards

- It is important to bear in mind that everything we publish on the internet can be replicated in a way which cannot be controlled.

1. Be truthful: sincerity is crucial. It is essential to be truthful and transparent. Untruths are very quickly found out.

2. Be careful: before taking part in any conversation on the internet, ask yourself whether your contribution is important. Sometimes silence is golden.

3. Add value to the conversation: always try to publish relevant content.

4. Be friendly: an overly formal tone can give rise to suspicion. The best thing is to write in the first person, using the kind of relaxed tone you would use in off-line conversation.

5. Write correctly: in writing, our spelling and grammar form part of our image. Avoid abbreviation and the pointless use of upper-case fonts.

How to act from the corporate point of view

What we should do:

1. If we are involved in any conversation, we should always reveal our identity (BBVA) and any other information which will help others to know that we are using a corporate medium. With these profiles, the BBVA profile can be used.

2. If we are coordinating profiles managed by external companies, we should be certain that the platform managers are being transparent in their relationship with us and with the users.

3. Don't forget rule number one: be truthful.

4. Be careful with messages directed to each interest group associated with the profile. A good idea is to draw up a document beforehand with the main messages to be broadcast or with the communication framework within which you have to work for each action.

5. Follow the rules of the public forums in which you take part.

6. Abide by the data protection rules.

What we shouldn't do:

1. A corporate profile must never be used to express personal opinions.

2. Intermediaries should never be used to express your opinions.

3. Never ask a blogger or platform manager to publish anything false or something that he doesn't believe.

4. Don't change the subject of the conversation (go "off-topic") to divert attention or to promote something.

5. Don't use spam techniques to publish comment.

6. Don't ask employees to broadcast messages with their personal profiles, unless it is necessary and justified.

Basic standards for responding to comment:

– Work out who or what will be affected by the comment: business, reputation, CSR, etc.

– Work out who or which department is the best place to respond: the ideal is that a response should come from whoever knows most about the subject.

– Always respond in a positive tone and add value to the conversation.

– Never respond to insults or rumours: an official response to a rumour might spread it.

What to do in a crisis situation:

The most important thing is to detect potential crises before they happen. As far as on-line communications are concerned, a global monitoring service is available, but in any case any employee can raise the alarm if he discovers a message which might directly affect BBVA's good name or business.

Procedure:

– Never respond to rumours, and certainly not immediately, as this will just help them to spread.

– If it is felt that the message detected is serious, quickly contact Global Corporate Communication before responding.

– Before evaluating the content of the message, its real impact must be assessed: very often he who speaks has no listeners, and a response might simply spread it.

– If it is felt that a response is required once the message has been analysed, then it must always be positive, must add value, and must be launched via the same channel that was used for the original message.

– The detection/consultation/possible response procedure should not exceed 30 minutes.

Security recommendations to be observed when opening a BBVA profile, page or group on social networks.

Creating pages/groups:

– An official pages/groups authorisation flow procedure should be set up. Even though this initiative may not involve technological developments or deployment, it is necessary to ensure that its viability and impact are adequately reviewed, including from the point of view of Information Security.

- The part of the content that has been provided by BBVA should be clearly identified, by means of the logos and possible style guides which Online Communication may have set up, and which part came from third parties, plus where liability does not apply.

- The objective and scope of the page/group/wiki/blog, etc. should be clearly indicated.

- Under no circumstances can they be used to provide banking services, or in-house management services, since these services must be channelled as initiatives via the appropriate Production Department/Business Partner.

- The administrators must be sure that the information included may be publicly distributed, is relevant, accurate and supplies no information subject to the protection of a personal nature, privileged stock market information, or information of any other kind which is subject to confidentiality by law, by regulations or by BBVA standards.

General recommendations for administrators:

- Always administer from the bank's teams (in the bank or remotely).

- Set up a robust password. The best idea is to choose a sentence which the administrator can remember and then use the first letter of each word.

- Never share the password with other individuals, and the password should be different from the personal email/page password.

- Pay special attention to such mechanisms as they may be used to remember the passwords of the question-and-answer style register.

Below, thanks to the generosity of CISCO for their contribution to this book, we share the Social Media Policy: " Cisco Social Media Best Practices".

1. **Be authentic and add value:** Use your real identity online. Express an interesting point of view, worthwhile information and unique perspective. When speaking about Cisco, offer your subject matter expertise, and if you are unsure about whether a topic is appropriate, submit a question on the Global Social Media Community discussion forum.

2. **Be responsible and honest:** You are personally responsible for the content you provide and how you behave on social media sites. We encourage you to participate online, but urge you to do so properly, exercising solid judgment. Always tell the truth. Correct any mistakes you make as quickly as possible. Don't alter older posts without indicating that you have done so.

3. **Be factual, respectful, and avoid engaging in online disputes:** Provide informed, well-supported opinions and cite sources, if applicable. Do not post content about the company or individuals that is vulgar, obscene, threatening, intimidating, defamatory, discriminatory, harassing or in violation of the company's policies against discrimination, harassment or hostility on account of age, race, religion, sex, ethnicity, nationality, disability or other protected class, status or characteristic. You should not unlawfully disparage the company's products or services.

4. **Be sensitive:** The lines between business and personal information have blurred, and not all customers realize that social data can be publicly available.

5. **Do not engage in inflammatory or inappropriate discussions about competitors:** If you have been approved

by your manager to talk about competitors externally, lead with Cisco's strengths and rely on facts and publicly available data. Do not cite or reference clients, partners, or suppliers without their approval. When you do make a reference, where possible link it back to the source. You should not unlawfully disparage the products or services of our vendors or competitors.

6. **Be mindful of the indefinite life of internet postings:** You should assume that all internet postings, including those posted in a private forum, can be made **public** and searchable indefinitely. Private discussions may inadvertently or intentionally get posted externally. Even if you "remove or delete" a posting from the original source, there is no way of knowing where it may have been reposted.

7. **Be aware of laws** covering defamation, insider trading, financial disclosures, endorsements and testimonials, antitrust, competition, privacy, and the protection of intellectual property.

8. **Build relationships:** Focus on engagement with the audience and building trust to develop relationships rather than using social media solely as a marketing tool to sell Cisco products or to promote yourself. It's important to build trust within your social networks before trying to sell.

9. **Review the privacy settings** of the social media site you are using. Choose social sites and settings that are appropriate for the content you are posting. Understand that when your content is posted on a public social network, all posts and comments may be traceable. Any information that you post should be considered at risk for public disclosure, regardless of your privacy settings because your postings can be reposted elsewhere and may be viewed by people other than your intended audience.

10. **Be aware of global implications:** Your posts can have global significance. The way that you answer an online question might be appropriate in some parts of the world, but inaccurate, inappropriate (or even illegal) in others. Keep that "world view" in mind when you participate in online conversations.

Coca-Cola has also set down some recommendations for its employees regarding the use of Twitter:

1. Be transparent: always reveal the employment relationship you have with the company.

2. Bear in mind the fact that comments you make at a local level may have global repercussions.

3. Don't forget that content uploaded onto the internet stays on the internet for ever.

4. If you are ever unsure about what you are about to write, the best thing is not to write it.

Some companies, such as Sainsbury's, have taken things further, and dictated an in-house self-regulation policy which prohibits any member of the company management from making use of the information published on the profiles of their employees on any social network.

The most popular social media discoveries made by online recruiters that lead to a candidate not getting a job. Source: http://www.statista.com (2016)

*   Candidate posted provocative/inappropriate photos or information: 46%

*   There was evidence of candidate drinking or using drugs: 41%

- Candidate had bad-mouthed previous employer: 36%

- Candidate had poor communication skills: 32%

- Candidate made discriminatory comments related to race, gender, religion or other topics: 28%

- Candidate had lied about his or her qualifications: 25%

- Candidate was linked to criminal behaviour: 22%

- Candidate's screen name was unprofessional: 21%

- Candidate lied about an absence: 13%

5

International HR Trends. Mobile Recruiting. Big Data. The Future of Work

5.1. Trends in social media at the international level

We must not expect things to change if we always do the same thing.

Albert Einstein

International panorama of social networks

According to We are Social's "Digital in 2016" report, the following statistics give an international point of view of the penetration of leading social networks and social media trends:

Social media trends in Argentina

Penetration of leading social networks in Argentina (2016) % Share of population:

Facebook: 42%
WhatsApp: 37%

Facebook Messenger: 29%
Google+: 20%
Twitter: 18%
Skype: 13%
Instagram: 13%
Taringa: 11%
LinkedIn: 10%
Pinterest: 8%

Social media trends in Australia

Penetration of leading social networks in Australia (2016) %
Share of population:

Facebook: 41%
Facebook Messenger: 26%
Skype: 13%
Google+: 11%
LinkedIn: 11%
Twitter: 10%
WhatsApp: 10%
Instagram: 10%
Pinterest: 9%
Tumblr: 6%

Social media trends in Brazil

Penetration of leading social networks in Brazil (2016) %
Share of population:

Facebook: 31%
WhatsApp: 29%
Facebook Messenger: 24%
Google+: 17%
Instagram: 15%
Skype: 15%
Twitter: 14%

LinkedIn: 12%
Snapchat: 9%
Pinterest: 8%

Social media trends in Canada

Penetration of leading social networks in Canada (2016) %
Share of population:

Facebook: 47%
Facebook Messenger: 28%
Twitter: 16%
Instagram: 14%
Google+: 13%
LinkedIn: 12%
Skype: 12%
Pinterest: 12%
WhatsApp: 10%
Snapchat: 10%

Social media trends in China

Penetration of leading social networks in China (2016) %
Share of population:

Wechat: 24%
QZone: 21%
Sina Weibo: 16%
Tencent Weibo: 12%
Renren: 6%
Facebook: 5%
Kaixin001: 5%
Facebook Messenger: 4%
51.com: 3%

Social media trends in France

Penetration of leading social networks in France (2016) % Share of population:

Facebook: 43%
Facebook Messenger: 22%
Google+: 11%
Twitter: 11%
Snapchat: 9%
Skype: 8%
WhatsApp: 7%
Instagram: 7%
LinkedIn: 6%
Pinterest: 5%

Social media trends in Germany

Penetration of leading social networks in Germany (2016) % Share of population:

WhatsApp: 39%
Facebook: 38%
Facebook Messenger: 20%
Skype: 10%
Google+: 9%
Instagram: 7%
Twitter: 7%
Pinterest: 4%
Snapchat: 4%
LinkedIn: 3%

Social media trends in Hong Kong

Penetration of leading social networks in Hong Kong (2016) % Share of population:

Facebook: 50%
WhatsApp: 47%
Facebook Messenger: 30%
WeChat: 24%
Instagram: 17%
Line: 17%
Google+: 15%
Skype: 10%
Sina Weibo: 9%
LinkedIn: 8%

Social media trends in India

Penetration of leading social networks in India (2016) % Share of population:

Facebook: 13%
WhatsApp: 12%
Facebook Messenger: 11%
Google+: 10%
Skype: 10%
Twitter: 8%
Hike Messenger: 8%
LinkedIn: 7%
Instragram: 7%
WeChat: 6%

Social media trends in Indonesia

Penetration of leading social networks in Indonesia (2016) % Share of population:

BBM: 19%
Facebook: 15%
WhatsApp: 14%
Facebook Messenger: 13%
Google+: 12%

Line: 12%
Twitter: 11%
Instagram: 10%
WeChat: 8%
Pinterest: 7%

Social media trends in Italy

Penetration of leading social networks in Italy (2016) % Share of population:

Facebook: 33%
WhatsApp: 30%
Facebook Messenger: 23%
Google+: 14%
Twitter: 12%
Instagram: 12%
Skype: 12%
LinkedIn: 9%
Pinterest: 6%
Viber: 6%

Social media trends in Japan

Penetration of leading social networks in Japan (2016) % Share of population:

Line: 25%
Facebook: 17%
Twitter: 15%
Mixi: 5%
Facebook Messenger: 3%
Ameblo: 3%
Instagram: 2%
Google+: 2%
Mobage: 2%
Gree: 1%

Social media trends in Malaysia

Penetration of leading social networks in Malaysia (2016) %
Share of population:

Facebook: 41%
WhatsApp: 39%
Facebook Messenger: 33%
Google+: 23%
WeChat: 23%
Instagram: 22%
Line: 17%
Twitter: 16%
Skype: 13%
LinkedIn: 11%

Social media trends in Mexico

Penetration of leading social networks in Mexico (2016) %
Share of population:

Facebook: 25%
WhatsApp: 23%
Facebook Messenger: 21%
Twitter: 16%
Google+: 15%
Skype: 13%
Instagram: 12%
Pinterest: 10%
LinkedIn: 9%
Tumblr: 9%

Social media trends in Poland

Penetration of leading social networks in Poland (2016) %
Share of population:

Facebook: 36%
Facebook Messenger: 19%
Google+: 14%
Skype: 10%
Twitter: 7%
Instagram: 6%
WhatsApp: 6%
NK.PL: 6%
LinkedIn: 5%
Gadu-Gadu: 5%

Social media trends in Russia

Penetration of leading social networks in Russia (2016) % Share of population:

VK: 39%
Odnoklassniki: 32%
Facebook: 24%
Skype: 19%
Google+: 17%
Viber: 15%
WhatsApp: 15%
Instagram: 12%
Twitter: 11%
Facebook Messenger: 6%

Social media trends in Saudi Arabia

Penetration of leading social networks in Saudi Arabia (2016) % Share of population:

WhatsApp: 27%
Facebook: 25%
Facebook Messenger: 20%
Twitter: 20%
Instagram: 17%

Google+: 15%
Skype: 14%
Snapchat: 13%
Line: 12%
LinkedIn: 11%

Social media trends in Singapore

Penetration of leading social networks in Singapore (2016) %
Share of population:

WhatsApp: 46%
Facebook: 43%
Facebook Messenger: 26%
Instagram: 18%
Google+: 14%
Line: 14%
LinkedIn: 14%
Skype: 13%
Twitter: 13%
WeChat: 12%

Social media trends in South Africa

Penetration of leading social networks in South Africa (2016)
% Share of population:

WhatsApp: 33%
Facebook: 30%
Facebook Messenger: 20%
Google+: 15%
LinkedIn: 13%
Twitter: 12%
Pinterest: 11%
Instagram: 10%
BBM: 9%
Skype: 9%

Social media trends in South Korea

Penetration of leading social networks in South Korea (2016) % Share of population:

KakaoTalk: 41%
Facebook: 27%
KakaoStory: 17%
Facebook Messenger: 12%
Twitter: 10%
Line: 7%
Instagram: 7%
Google+: 6%
Twitch: 4%
Tumblr: 3%

Social media trends in Spain

Penetration of leading social networks in Spain (2016) % Share of population:

WhatsApp: 45%
Facebook: 44%
Facebook Messenger: 24%
Twitter: 24%
Google+: 21%
Instagram: 15%
LinkedIn: 14%
Skype: 13%
Pinterest: 9%
Line: 8%

Social media trends in Taiwan

Penetration of leading social networks in Taiwan (2016) % Share of population:

Facebook: 41%
LINE: 33%
Facebook Messenger: 25%
Google+: 17%
Skype: 16%
WeChat: 10%
Twitter: 9%
WhatsApp: 6%
Instagram: 6%
Plurk: 5%

Social media trends in The Philippines

Penetration of leading social networks in The Philippines (2016) % Share of population:

Facebook: 26%
Facebook Messenger: 23%
Google+: 17%
Skype: 16%
Viber: 14%
Twitter: 13%
Instagram: 12%
LinkedIn: 11%
Pinterest: 9%
WeChat: 9%

Social media trends in Thailand

Penetration of leading social networks in Thailand (2016) % Share of population:

Facebook: 32%
Line: 29%
Facebook Messenger: 28%
Google+: 22%
Instagram: 19%

Twitter: 14%
Pinterest: 11%
WhatsApp: 11%
Skype: 10%
LinkedIn: 10%

Social media trends in Turkey

Penetration of leading social networks in Turkey (2016) %
Share of population:

Facebook: 32%
WhatsApp: 24%
Facebook Messenger: 20%
Twitter: 17%
Instagram: 16%
Google+: 15%
Skype: 13%
LinkedIn: 9%
Viber: 8%
Vine: 7%

Social media trends in the United Arab Emirates

Penetration of leading social networks in the United Arab
Emirates (2016) % Share of population:

WhatsApp: 47%
Facebook: 46%
Skype: 46%
Facebook Messenger: 42%
Twitter: 29%
Instagram: 27%
LinkedIn: 27%
Google+: 27%
Viber: 20%
Snapchat: 19%

Social media trends in the UK

Penetration of leading social networks in the UK (2016) % Share of population:

Facebook: 47%
Facebook Messenger: 32%
WhatsApp: 24%
Twitter: 20%
Instagram: 14%
Skype: 13%
Snapchat: 12%
Google+: 10%
LinkedIn: 10%
Pinterest: 8%

Social media trends in the United States

Penetration of leading social networks in the United States (2016) % Share of population:

Facebook: 41%
Facebook Messenger: 26%
Twitter: 17%
Pinterest: 15%
Instagram: 15%
Google+: 12%
LinkedIn: 11%
Snapchat: 11%
Skype: 9%
Tumblr: 8%

Social media trends in Vietnam

Penetration of leading social networks in Vietnam (2016) % Share of population:

Facebook: 29%
Zalo: 25%
Facebook Messenger: 25%
Google+: 20%
Skype: 15%
Viber: 11%
Line: 10%
Twitter: 9%
Instagram: 15%
WhatsApp: 6%

Online recruitment users, by industry, in the U.S. are as follows:

- Information Technology
- Finance & Banking
- Healthcare
- Manufacturing
- Engineering
- Sales
- Admin & Clerical
- Telecommunications
- Biotech & Pharma
- Staffing & Recruiting
- Source: http://www.statista.com

5.2. Mobile Recruiting

One billion job searches are carried out each month from a mobile device and 45% of active candidates apply for a job through their mobile device.

The number of active mobile connections surpassed the total world population.

With mobile-oriented services like WhatsApp, WeChat and Facebook Messenger achieving the top social media ranking spots in some of the world's biggest economies, it is clear that much of our digital behaviour is now converging around mobile devices.

According to the "Social Recruitment Survey" by Jobvite:

Mobile usage is empowering job seekers to look for jobs more openly: 41% in bed, 38% during their commute, 36% in a restaurant, 30% at work and 18% in the restroom.

There's a mobile disconnect between job seekers and recruiters:

Despite 43% of job seekers using mobile devices in their job search, 59% of recruiters currently invest nothing in mobile career sites.

For those who are leveraging the power of mobile usage, they are already seeing its impact on candidate engagement:

- Improves time-to-hire: 14%

- Improves quality of candidate: 13%

- Improves quantity of hires: 19%

- Improves quality/quantity of referrals: 10%

Some mobile recruitment statistics:

- 20% of recruiters have a mobile-optimized career site.

- 37% of Millennial job seekers expect career websites to be optimized for a mobile device.

- 5% of Fortune 500 companies allow job seekers to apply from a mobile device.

- 13% of recruiters say they have invested enough in mobile recruiting efforts.

- 62% of passive job seekers will explore a company's career page on a mobile device.

- 40% of mobile candidates abandon a non-mobile friendly application process.

- Active job seekers look for opportunities almost equally on job sites (71%) and social networks (69%).

- In a survey LinkedIn ran, 28% of respondents were active job seekers.

- 61% of people have a better impression of a brand based on their mobile experience.

- 62% of recruiters say #mobile #recruiting is the top trend for 2014.

- 71% access social media via a mobile device.

- 50% of emails are opened on mobile devices.

- 50% of cell phone owners download apps to their mobile device.

- Users globally spend nearly 3 hours daily on their mobile devices.

- On average, Americans spend 2.7 hours per day socializing on their mobile devices. In Europe, the average is 2.4 hours. In Asia Pac, the average is 3.4 hours.

- 61% of people have a better impression of a brand based on their mobile experience.

According to the survey "The Corporate Mobile Readiness Report":

The Corporate Mobile Readiness Report is an on-going study of the Fortune 500 regarding their preparations for the rapidly increasing shift toward the use of mobile devices by candidates to search for and apply for jobs.

This survey considers the following metrics to evaluate if a company is adapted or not to mobile recruitment:

– Mobile Optimized Corporate Site: The content on the homepage of the corporate website must be displayed in a format that is appropriately sized to the screen of the device.

– Careers Link: The corporate site must be optimized and there must be a careers or jobs link found on the site.

– Mobile Optimized Career Section: The content on the career section must be displayed in a format that is appropriately sized to the screen of the device, and must include functionality to search and browse job opportunities.

– Mobile Optimized Apply Process: The job seeker must be able to complete the entire application process from the mobile device.

– Optimized pages.

– Redirect: All links to career related content from search results lists or the corporate site must redirect the job seeker to mobile optimized pages of content.

– Other Career Content: The mobile optimized career site provides career related content other than the jobs, such as About Us, Benefits, etc.

- Native App: There must be a company branded SmartPhone or Tablet app found in the app store. The purpose of the app may be for business or careers.

The survey highlighted the following top eight companies with the best Corporate Mobile Readiness Index (CMRI) score:

- AT&T

- Dow Chemical

- General Motors

- Macy's

- McDonalds

- Walmart

- Casey's General Stores

- Tyson Foods

For example: If you look at the McDonald's mobile app you will notice that their recruiting team managed to insert a Careers tab front and center as the app opens. Injecting a careers option in your already existing company app is a great way to save money and reach a wide audience.

According to the "Social Recruitment survey" by Jobvite:

- 55% of recruiters use or plan to use a mobile career site to support recruiting efforts.

- Recruiters are already seeing the benefits with improved time-to-hire (14%) and quality of candidates (13%).

Graylink http://www.graylink.biz announced the launch of txthire in the UK market, which enables job application and screening via SMS, social media, instant messaging, web and .mobi channels. This unique interactive tool won the Gartner 2011 Cool Vendor Award for Graylink and is just one of a leading edge suite of mobile and web recruitment solutions which the company offers.

Txthire is secure, cloud-based software for recruitment process mobilization.

- Enables candidates to apply with any mobile device – txthire supports SMS, mobile internet, social media & IM channels.

- Automatically pre-screens and scores applicants using job-specific questionnaire's.

- Exchanges applicant data with external systems.

- Interfaces with your ERP, HRM and/or ATS or uses as a stand-alone service.

According with Michael Marlatt, a recruiting consultant for Microsoft:

"In less than 30 years, the mobile industry has become the fastest growing trillion dollar industry. But for all its power, the recruitment industry has stayed relatively quiet on the mobile recruiting front. It's Web 1.0 all over again, but this time with mobile. Who aren't positioning mobile as a top-tier source for candidates are missing out on a powerful resource. Any company exploring new ways for attracting and engaging diversity talent should not overlook this untapped channel."

Mobile recruiting capability is no longer an option for employers, it is a requirement. Though mobile devices are a tool and not a source, job seekers around the globe use them 24/7 to find positions and engage with prospective companies.

Industry research shows that it is simply good business to make mobile a central part of a recruitment strategy: In the

U.S. alone, 64% of adults now own a smartphone of some kind. Of those, 43% used their phones in the past year to look up a job.

> *"The common mistake is to see mobile recruitment as a one-time investment. Our biggest success is the fact that we made mobile recruitment part of our organic growth."*
>
> Vildan Stidham (Abbott)

Some recommendations to optimize in the use of a corporate app for recruitment:

- Filter jobs by function and department.

- Be sure your web page is responsive: the search works on a mobile device.

- Keep your job descriptions short and to-the-point.

Some of the benefits to implementing Mobile Recruiting policies are the engagement of the potential candidates (Staying in touch with them through quick text messages, emails or phone calls) and hiring managers. It provides an innovative on-site candidate experience.

HR organizations must allocate a budget to enable recruiting systems for "small screen applications" and all types of handheld devices. Otherwise, recruiters risk losing candidates to their more tech-savvy competitors.

5.3. Big Data and the future of HR

> *We have entered a global economy where talent and skills shortages challenge world economic and business growth around the world.*
>
> Klaus Schwab, Chairman, World Economic Forum

As technology continues to shape our businesses, our role evolves to that of a more proactive strategic partner, a greater critical change agent and a bigger culture champion.

Technology has the power to turn annual performance reviews into immediate feedback, while recognition programs can become online platforms. Technology will also usher in a new era for accessible training that can be taken anywhere, anytime, in any language; while virtual resumes and interviews will become the norm. Employees will use apps to find out about their work, their total rewards, their schedules and more.

A recent study by influential HR thinker David Ulrich and executive recruiting firm Korn Ferry shows the CHRO role is more important than ever before. As Ulrich said in modern business, attracting the right talent, creating the right organizational structure and building the right culture are essential for driving strategy.

What is Big Data?

Big Data analytics requires people who are knowledgeable about the business, who think creatively around insights and patterns, and who have the methodologies and tools that provide insights to help inform decisions.

David Hom, Principal at Deloitte Consulting

Big Data is a term used to describe the new volume, variety and velocity of data. Organizations must recognize that Big Data is a tool to provide new or better insight. It is an enabler. Initially, most organizations hire "data scientists" to gather data and explore questions.

As the experts point out, Big Data initiatives are characterized by three criteria:

1. Volume (the data sets used are enormous)

2. Variety (data streaming in from a vast number of sources)

3. Velocity (the increased pace at which data is being created and then incorporated into the analytic process and the ability to put the data to use in real time as it streams in)

According to a recent study by Deloitte: By using Big Data analytics solutions, and specifically high-performance analytics, businesses and governments can analyse huge amounts of data in seconds and minutes to reveal previously unseen patterns, sentiments and customer intelligence. This speed and accuracy of insight, delivered across any device including smart phones and tablets, means organisations can make better, faster decisions.

- IBM has calculated that 90% of all the digital data has been created in the last two years.

- The *New York Times* has published 2.9 billion words since 1959. Twitter publishes 8 billion words per day, Facebook 10 billion.

- A major part of this shift is the explosion in new tools. Today nearly every major HR software vendor (Oracle, SAP, ADP, Ceridian, Workday as well as specialty companies like SumTotal, Cornerstone, Lumesse, Silkroad, Ultimate, and hundreds of others) are building and buying end-to-end HR suites, very similarly to the evolution of customer relationship marketing. Today Oracle (OBIA), SAP (Workforce Intelligence), Workday (Big Data Analytics), and SumTotal have all launched major integrated HR analytics systems.

- 71% of CEOs view human capital as the top factor contributing to sustainable economic value.

- 43% of CEOs indicated that investing in HR is a high priority.

- #1 Big Data Challenge: Sharing information across silos.

Big Data: The Keys to Success

1. Reliable

   - Data must be "true" and validated over time

   - Seasonal changes, organization changes, must be handled

2. Actionable

   - Reports must be detailed enough to let managers take action

   - Drill, filter, group data so it is relevant and meaningful

   - Goal is a "business-driven" dashboard (red/yellow/green)

3. Scalable

   - The process of collecting and analyzing data must scale

   - Your outputs must be useful for people at all levels

4. Understandable

   - People must be able to visualize and understand what you find

   - Line managers, executives and employees must use the data

Big Data in HR

The old fashioned fuddy-duddy HR department is changing. The Geeks have arrived. Today, for the first time in the 15 years I've been an analyst, human resources departments are getting serious about analytics. And I mean serious.

Josh Bersin, Principal and Founder. Bersin By Deloitte

Big Data in HR will allow us to move beyond a simple headcount and be more predictive than reactionary. We have to move from being pure HR experts to business experts who use analytics to drive our actions.

The future trend of HR professionals will be using analytics to continuously learn from historical trends and impending talent needs in order to determine where to focus and how to optimize talent programs.

A recent global survey of executives at more than 1,200 companies by Tata Consulting Services confirmed that finance and HR are among the lowest priorities for Big Data investment.

According to the LinkedIn survey "Global Recruiting Trends":

- 24% of global recruiting leaders believe they are using data very well in their roles.

- Recruiting leaders need to strengthen their talent analytics capabilities to stay ahead.

- The best 10 countries using Big Data in HR are: India, MENA, Southeast Asia, Brazil, Mexico, United States, South Africa, Canada, China and Spain.

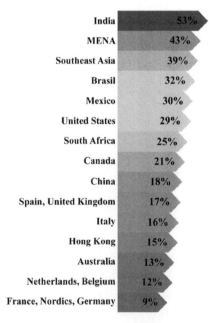

India	53%
MENA	43%
Southeast Asia	39%
Brasil	32%
Mexico	30%
United States	29%
South Africa	25%
Canada	21%
China	18%
Spain, United Kingdom	17%
Italy	16%
Hong Kong	15%
Australia	13%
Netherlands, Belgium	12%
France, Nordics, Germany	9%

Here are some Big Data scenarios that blend finance and HR, and that could grow out of a technologically and globally integrated enterprise.

- Analyze global payroll costs.

- Determine the profitability of individual customers.

- Gain a complete picture of an organization's staffing.

- Use advanced visualization techniques on geospatial data.

- Analyze the impact of wellness programs on employees.

- Less than 25% of CHROs are using analytics to make future workforce decisions.

- Only 6% of HR departments believe they are "excellent" in analytics and more than 60% feel they are poor or behind.

Other purposes for HR departments:

- Identify potential recruits

- Measure costs per hire and return on investment

- Measure employee productivity

- Measure the impact of HR programs on performance

- Identify (and predict) attrition rates and new hire failure rates

- Identify potential leaders

The key is that the profile of the business partner must change. Even in senior HRBPs the reaction to anything to do with data and process is horror. We have got to shake and break this, as it would not be tolerated anywhere else in business.

The true HR pro of the future has got to be a great project manager, business person and analyst and be able to negotiate and influence. But currently an awful lot of them do not fit the bill even at senior levels.

The Chartered Institute of Personnel and Development (CIPD) recently announced that talent analytics and Big Data are now must-have capabilities in HR.

If an HR function can target human capital investment with precision and anticipate future issues, then there will be less waste due to poor decision-making and better investments in proactive HR interventions.

HR Big Data could prepare companies for transparency, helping them make sense of a complex interconnected world and giving them insights to drive the appropriate people strategy. Websites like glassdoor.com "the TripAdvisor for job search" mean outsiders, such as prospective employees and competitors, can see deep inside a company.

As a conclusion Big Data has a massive opportunity for HR so long as we follow nine golden rules:

1. Drive your data analytics from the business issue not the data.

2. Don't be seduced by the tools and technology; focus on people's ability to use them to address business issues.

3. Don't overinvest in your data initiative; start small and prove the concept.

4. Join your HR data with your finance, marketing, risk and other data.

5. Don't worry too much where your data analytics team sits but make sure they are connecting the data to the business issues and the HR solutions.

6. How you present the data is as important as the data – insightful, impactful, simple and relevant.

7. This will change HR so recruit HR people who get it: commercial, action oriented, focused, willing to challenge, agile and curious.

8. Develop data comfort in the whole HR function.

9. Data is a tool, not the answer; never lose track of the human element in HR.

Warning: before embarking on a Big Data initiative, be sure to know where your organizational culture sits on the spectrum.

In a "negative" sense, any initiative using HR data will be received as too much "Big Brother" and be seen as a weapon to control and punish, and also be viewed as a loss of privacy.

In a more "positive" sense, it will be seen as a tool to help improve the organization's effectiveness and boost productivity – something that is part of the organizational learning journey and that will improve employee engagement.

You have to have a leader who's committed to changing the minds of the rest of the executive suite that HR is important and an enabler for everything else in the organization.

Harry Osle, Global HR Transformation and Advisory practice leader, The Hackett Group

Big data is essential to HR and L&D because it allows the conversations and connections, which have tended to be in the realm of the immeasurable, to be captured and leveraged.

Gartner's three V's of Big Data: Volume, Velocity, Variety.

VOLUME

Every second more data crosses the Web than was present across the whole internet in 1993. Cloud offers massive increase in storage.

VELOCITY

Faster data at higher speeds than ever before, even in remote locations.
Real-time data.

VARIETY

More data on more aspects of life and work on a greater range of devices and channels, from smartphones to embedded chips.

The three S's of talent analytics and Big Data in HR: Silos, Skills, Suspicion.

SILOS

Structural and system obstacles to HR's and others' effective and consistent use of data which can enable or impede a data-driven HR strategy.

SKILLS

The extent of analytical skills, smarts and talent which helps support a data-driven HR strategy.

SUSPICION

Mindsets and cultures around data and its role in HR which can help or hinder a data-driven HR strategy.

It's clear that companies around the world are making a big investment in Big Data. *The Wall Street Journal* recently reported that 85% of Fortune 1000 executives have projects planned or underway for getting more business value out of data their companies generate and collect. And a recent Gartner report projects that Big Data will account for 28 billion U.S. dollars of IT spending globally this year and will increase to 34 billion U.S. dollars in 2013.

Big Data offers an historic opportunity: the opportunity to make the most rigorously evidence-based human capital decisions ever made.

5.4. The future of work

For a talent 3.0. revolution to take place, governments and businesses will need to profoundly change their approach to education, skills and employment, and their approach to working with each other. Businesses will need to put talent development and future workforce strategy front and centre to their growth. They require a new mindset to meet their talent needs and to optimize social outcomes. As the issue becomes more urgent, governments will need to show bolder leadership in putting through the curricula and labour market regulation changes that are already decades overdue in some economies.

Timeframe to impact industries, business models

Impact felt already	2015–2017	2018–2020
» Rising geopolitical volatility	» New energy supplies and technologies	» Advanced robotics and autonomous transport
» Mobile internet and cloud technology	» The Internet of Things	» Artificial intelligence and machine learning
» Advances in computing power and Big Data	» Advanced manufacturing and 3D printing	» Advanced materials, biotechnology and genomics
» Crowdsourcing, the sharing economy and peer-to-peer platforms	» Longevity and ageing societies	
» Rise of the middle class in emerging markets	» New consumer concerns about ethical and privacy issues	
» Young demographics in emerging markets	» Women's rising aspirations and economic power	
» Rapid urbanization		
» Changing work environments and flexible working arrangements		
» Climate change, natural resource constraints and the transition to a greener economy		

According to the World Economic Forum (2016):

It is therefore critical that broader and longer term changes to basic and lifelong education systems are complemented with specific, urgent and focused re-skilling efforts in each industry. This entails several major changes in how business views and manages talent, both immediately and in the longer term. In particular, the Future of Jobs Report finds that there are four areas with short-term implications and three that are critical for long-term resilience.

Immediate Focus

- **Reinventing the HR function:** As business leaders begin to consider proactive adaptation to the new talent landscape, they need to manage skills disruption as an urgent concern. What this requires is an HR function that is rapidly becoming more strategic and has a seat at the table—one that employs new kinds of analytical tools to spot talent trends and skills gaps, and provides insights that can help organizations align their business, innovation and talent management strategies to maximize available opportunities to capitalize on transformational trends.

- **Making use of data analytics:** Businesses and governments will need to build a new approach to workforce planning and talent management, where better forecasting data and planning metrics will need to be central. To support such efforts, the Forum's Future of Jobs project provides in-depth analysis on industries, countries, occupations and skills.

- **Talent diversity:** As study after study demonstrates the business benefits of workforce diversity and companies expect finding talent for many key specialist roles to become much more difficult by 2020, it is time for a fundamental change in how talent diversity issues are perceived and well-known barriers tackled. In this area, too, technology and data analytics may become a useful tool for advancing workforce parity, whether by facilitating objective assessment, identifying unconscious biases in job ads and recruitment processes or even by using wearable technologies to understand workplace behaviours and encourage systemic change.

- **Leveraging flexible working arrangements and online talent platforms**: As physical and organizational boundaries are becoming increasingly blurred, organizations are going to have to become significantly more agile in the way they think about managing people's work and about the workforce as a whole. Businesses will increasingly connect and collaborate remotely with freelancers and independent professionals through digital talent platforms. Modern forms of association such as digital freelancers' unions and updated labour market regulations will increasingly begin to emerge to complement these new organizational models.

Longer Term Focus

- ***Rethinking education systems:*** Most existing education systems at all levels provide highly siloed training and continue a number of 20th century practices that are hindering progress on today's talent and labour market issues. Two such legacy issues burdening formal education systems worldwide are the dichotomy between Humanities and Sciences and applied and pure training, on the one hand, and the prestige premium attached to tertiary-certified forms of education—rather than the actual content of learning— on the other hand. Businesses should work closely with governments, education providers and others to imagine what a true 21st century curriculum might look like.

- ***Incentivizing lifelong learning:*** The dwindling future population share of today's youth in many ageing economies implies that simply reforming current education systems to better equip today's students to meet future skills requirements —as worthwhile and daunting as that task is— is not going to be enough to remain competitive. Ageing countries won't just need lifelong learning —they will need wholesale reskilling of existing workforces throughout their lifecycle. Governments and businesses have many opportunities to collaborate more to ensure that individuals have the time, motivation and means to seek retraining opportunities.

- *Cross-industry and public-private collaboration:* Given the complexity of the change management needed, businesses will need to realize that collaboration on talent issues, rather than competition, is no longer a nice-to-have but rather a necessary strategy. Multi-sector partnerships and collaboration, when they leverage the expertise of each partner in a complementary manner, are indispensable components of implementing scalable solutions to jobs and skills challenges. There is thus a need for bolder leadership and strategic action within companies and within and across industries, including partnerships with public institutions and the education sector.

Net employment outlook by job family, 2015–2020
Employees (thousands, all focus countries)

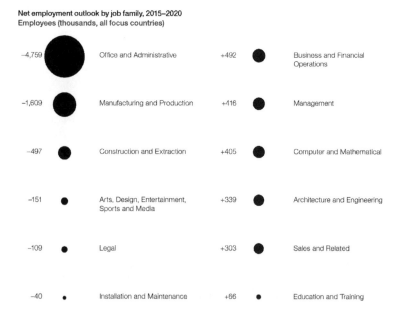

−4,759	Office and Administrative	+492	Business and Financial Operations
−1,609	Manufacturing and Production	+416	Management
−497	Construction and Extraction	+405	Computer and Mathematical
−151	Arts, Design, Entertainment, Sports and Media	+339	Architecture and Engineering
−109	Legal	+303	Sales and Related
−40	Installation and Maintenance	+66	Education and Training

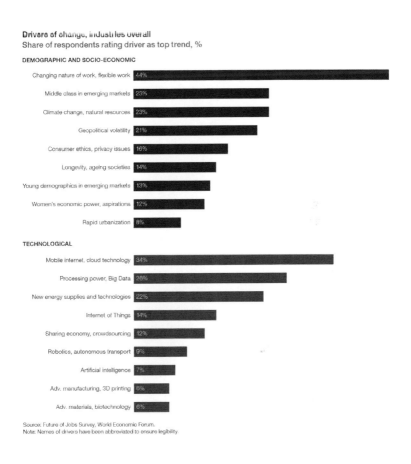

Drivers of change, industries overall
Share of respondents rating driver as top trend, %

DEMOGRAPHIC AND SOCIO-ECONOMIC

Changing nature of work, flexible work	44%
Middle class in emerging markets	23%
Climate change, natural resources	23%
Geopolitical volatility	21%
Consumer ethics, privacy issues	16%
Longevity, ageing societies	14%
Young demographics in emerging markets	13%
Women's economic power, aspirations	12%
Rapid urbanization	8%

TECHNOLOGICAL

Mobile internet, cloud technology	34%
Processing power, Big Data	26%
New energy supplies and technologies	22%
Internet of Things	14%
Sharing economy, crowdsourcing	12%
Robotics, autonomous transport	9%
Artificial intelligence	7%
Adv. manufacturing, 3D printing	6%
Adv. materials, biotechnology	6%

Source: Future of Jobs Survey, World Economic Forum.
Note: Names of drivers have been abbreviated to ensure legibility.

Conclusions

Companies wishing to attract and select talent must adapt to new technologies and social networks.

Companies must boost the efforts they are making to attract and develop talent since the future will belong to people who are multidisciplinary, multicultural, creative and involved. Businesses will increasingly need multi-skilled personnel, capable of coping with challenges in different departments and different countries. The candidate of today might be in any corner of the world, and we must be able to reach out to him. Social networks will bring that talent to us, and they represent a living, dynamic environment, and it is we who must change to fit with it.

Looking for a job is a process with many facets: we must make use of all the tools available.

The use of the ICTs in the recruitment process is changing the ways candidates are sought, making companies adopt a more active attitude than they have for years.

The new Generation of Talent (Generation Y) will represent 85% of the workforce worldwide.

Transparency is needed as the engine of change and the construction of open, collaborative companies, organisations which grow because people make them grow. We must reinvent formal structures, and that may mean they cease to be hierarchical and become "net-archical".

The future is being built by each and every one of us, and in a society, which is increasingly open, transparent and hyper-connected we are the ones who must take the role of the protagonist. In the wake of the revolutions we have experienced, we are now in the throes of a social revolution, since never before has technology been so important to people of every generation and culture.

HR must excel at innovation in order to deal effectively with these 21st-century talent gaps.

The challenge is also to have world-class HR expertise that can implement the best practices in recruiting, retaining, and developing global talent on a local basis.

Big Data will be a trend in HR and the demand for Big Data expertise is growing every day as companies become aware of the benefits of collecting and analyzing data. Currently the number of people specialized in Big Data trained to analyse this data isn't growing in line with the high demand. This creates a challenge for companies looking to hire experts, and who need to adapt to the new global talent management

As automation technologies such as machine learning and robotics play an increasingly greater role in everyday life, their potential effect on the workplace has, become a major focus of public concern. But which jobs will or won't be replaced by machines? According to McKinsey: technical feasibility and the cost of developing and deploying both the hardware and the software for automation are both a necessary precondition for automation, but not a complete predictor that an activity will be automated. McKinsey demonstrated in a recent report that technologies could automate 45% of the activities people are paid to perform and that about 60% of all occupations could see 30% or more of their constituent activities automated, again with technologies available today.

We are facing a new paradigm characterised by dynamism and uncertainty, one in which the old models of the past will not work in a future which is almost upon us, and that means that our future will depend on our attitude to change. As Darwin said, "We have to adapt."

About the Author

 CEO at Global Human Capital Group (GHCG), an international HR Consulting firm that provides strategic solutions for human capital of international organizations. Associate Professor at Master in Work, Organizational, and Personnel Psychology (WOP-P). Director Postgraduate Human Capital 2.0. Professor Master Human Resources Management.

Author of two Spanish management books *El talento está en la red* (LID 2011) and co-author of *Los mitos de Silvia* (LID 2013).

Her professional career has been recognized in the book *Personalities of Spain* (2012), that includes the Spanish Ranking Top 50 business leaders and her HR career has been recognized in the Spanish Ranking of Top10 HR Business Experts (2011).

Over 24 years work experience as HR Head Director and Talent Management in Financial Institutions such as Citigroup where she was responsible for setting up the headquarters for Southern Europe, managing 14 countries with 1,500 employees of 50 different nationalities; and IT companies as a Member of the Executive Committee in Unit4 and Human Resources Director for Spain, Portugal and Africa.

23

years

building on our success

- 1993 Madrid
- 2007 Barcelona
- 2008 México DF y Monterrey
- 2010 Londres
- 2011 Nueva York y Buenos Aires
- 2012 Bogotá
- 2014 Shanghái y San Francisco